CHANNEL ISLANDS PILOT

MALCOLM ROBSON

NAUTICAL

See page 18 for a full description of these charts.
(See inside back cover to complete tidal cycle.)

For Treslyn
With love from Margaret
Happy sailing 1991.

Fourth edition 1990
published by Nautical Books
an imprint of
A & C Black (Publishers) Ltd
35 Bedford Row, London WC1R 4JH

First edition 1976.
Second edition 1979.
Third edition 1985.

© R.C.C. Pilotage Foundation 1990

ISBN 0 7136 5771 5

A CIP catalogue record for this book
is available from the British Library.

Caution

While great care has been taken in the compilation
of this book, it is regretted that neither author nor
publisher can accept responsibility for any
inaccuracies or mishaps arising from the work.

Filmset by August Filmsetting, Haydock, St Helens.
Printed in Great Britain at the St Edmundsbury Press
Bury St Edmunds, Suffolk.

Contents

Also available from Nautical by
Malcolm Robson:

French Pilot Volume 1: *Omonville to Treguier*
French Pilot Volume 2: *Port Blanc to Ile de Sein*
French Pilot Volume 3: *Raz de Sein to Belle Ile*
French Pilot Volume 4: *Morbihan to the Gironde*

Other RCC Pilotage Foundation Pilot Books

The Atlantic Crossing Guide	Adlard Coles
North Biscay Pilot	Adlard Coles (new edition May 1990)
North Brittany Pilot	Adlard Coles
Atlantic Spain and Portugal	Imray, Laurie, Norie and Wilson
The Atlantic Islands	Imray, Laurie, Norie and Wilson
The Azores, Madeira, Canaries and Cape Verde	

Acknowledgements

Unaided, no single person could possibly research a book like this. Fishermen, pilots, yachtsmen and harbour staff all freely gave help. I can remember when pilot marks were kept in those little books with a clasp and lock, and the only way was to go out in a boat and start looking for rocks.

My grateful thanks go to Harbourmasters and their staff: in Alderney to Jack Quinain and Dave Peacock; in Guernsey, it was Roddy Ray; Graeme Mercier, Stan Palmer and Brian Nibbs were the Jersey experts. The note-taking, typing, checking, sounding – all the unglamorous jobs – were cheerfully done by my wife, Joan.

My sketch charts are based on Admiralty charts, with the sanction of HM Stationery Office and of the Hydrographer of the Navy.

The photographs included are by permission of the Chief Pleas of Sark and Aerofilms, States of Jersey Tourism Committee, States of Alderney Tourist Committee and States of Guernsey Tourist Board.

Malcolm Robson
Sark, 1990

The RCC Pilotage Foundation

With the 4th edition of this book, the Pilotage Foundation of the Royal Cruising Club is beginning its' association with Malcolm Robson's work and his unique approach to the problems of pilotage. The Pilotage Foundation, which is a charitable foundation established by an American member of the Club to advance the education of the general public in the science of navigation and safety at sea, has undertaken the revision of major pilot books and has sponsored new ones where a requirement has been established. Malcolm Robson has generously given the copyright of his pilot books to the Foundation and it is the intention of the Foundation to maintain them in their particular style.

O. H. Robinson
Director

Introduction

'My god ... all those rocks ... and those terrific tides!' Isn't this the reaction by any yachtsman thinking of sailing to the Channel Islands? And also by many who have lived here all their lives, for of course it's all true. We do have big tides. There are plenty of rocks. But tides to be used: with all sails pulling hard but against a five-knot current, why not drop anchor and make the tea? In a couple of hours you can hoist sails again and instead of standing still, be covering the bottom at ten knots. As for those rocks, look on them as faithful friends – they don't move or change shape – and if there was 7ft here in great, great grandfather's time, that's all we want to know. 'Tide tables? What for you want dem tings? There are the rocks, they tells you all you want, them!' So said a Serquais once to me.

But just a little humility, a small respect for the Channel Islands is no bad thing. Do not feel ashamed to anchor in fog. If those marks don't quite seem to fit, stop and verify – you may be in the wrong channel. Mental sums like $6·7 - 1·3 + 1·7 + 28$ minutes may indicate 2 feet under your keel, but have you thought about an east wind and the barometer, and are you on the right page of the tide tables? A local pilot, at full speed, in broad daylight, recently hit a rock he had seen and passed 2600 times – familiarity breeds carelessness. Should you be belting down the Swinge on a spring ebb and meet a seagull flying backward, don't wait to get squinched in the overfalls – turn back – cheat the lifeboat!

For cruising among the islands any one boat is no better than another, but if you have a deep-keeled yacht you will be sadly restricted without legs. Obviously many marks can only be followed under power – 4 or 5 knots is plenty – so be sure your engine won't get temperamental in among those tombstones. Is your anchor bent on and ready on deck? A fisherman is as good as a plough, but don't let go in 15 fathoms with a 6-knot stream; you may have to wait for slack water – if you don't get pulled under. For a picnic stop close in among the rocks, buoy the anchor with a tripping line or, better, use a weight instead – it won't wedge between boulders.

Most of the marks have been sailed in our 44ft sloop *Hephzibah* which draws 2·1m – yes, she's still afloat – and you will see that I have drawn only a single contour on my charts, 3m. Anything below that isn't our concern, except where an anchorage is shown. How much each side of a given transit is safe is something you will have to judge from the Admiralty chart or from my sketch charts. Only occasionally have I stressed this side or the other. When going along using a stern mark, it is not only pointless but dangerous to look only ahead. After a check to see there are no lobster pots, other boats, etc., in the way, turn away and concentrate on the transit. Either you trust my marks or you don't.

Almost all Channel Islands pilotage depends on marks. A mark can be a house, a beacon, a church. It can also mean a transit, i.e. 'The mark for clearing le Bouc is Dinan × la Parquette.' Two objects in line form a 'mark'. Note the multiplication sign '×' which is used, to avoid confusion instead of the word 'by'. There are channel marks with rocks either side: clearance marks with a danger one side. Striking marks are what pilots have to learn; usually there are two for each rock – A × B and N × M. Where the two transits cross each other, there right underneath, is The Rock. A Breast mark is a secondary transit roughly abeam of a ship's course.

The word 'tide' is used in several ways. A 'fair tide' is a favourable current; a 'big tide' or 'neap tide' refers to the tidal height. 'Enough tide' is about depth. A feature of Channel Islands tides is the expression 'half tide'. Because of the large range and the big difference between springs and neaps it is convenient to refer to a height independent of either. Half tide doesn't vary more than 0·5m from the mean value – have you noticed the number of rocks called 'Demi' (half)?

The charts are simplified and so much has been left out that they must be treated for what they really are – sketch chartlets. I think elevations are possibly more important, which is why I show a view for almost every transit. If there isn't a view, it is either because the transit is an obvious one, or an unimportant one, or it isn't possible to find any suitable marks. Can I remind art critics that I am a sort of seaman, not an artist; try struggling with wet paper, holding the boat long enough on the marks, watching the sounder, shouting into a tape recorder, all at once. Then repeat the whole thing again because it's too late on the tide, again because it's too early on the tide, then again since there's too much wind, too much swell, or it's too hazy to see the marks.

On a chart, 'Bn W' doesn't convey much help when anxiously peering to windward in gathering dusk, so I have separately sketched many buoys and beacons. Which brings me to the IALA Buoyage – well, it may be international in other parts but here we seem to be more individual, don't we? Vive la différence.

Finally, whilst information has been checked, sorted and rechecked, an error could creep in. Neither the publisher or myself can be held responsible for mistakes. Please, please if you find any errors, or you can supply omissions, could you tell me?

Most of the marks have been sailed over in our 44ft sloop
Hephzibah

7

Charts and Marks

All mention of charts in this book means the sketch charts A–Z indexed in Fig. 2. These are metric sketch charts on which all drying heights, soundings, elevations have been reduced to LAT (Lowest Astronomical Tides). Liberties have been taken by extending both the LAT and the single sounding contour (3m) so as to envelop collective dangers. Bearings are True; those of all lights from seaward; of transits looking toward the marks. Symbols used are those in Admiralty symbol chart 5011 – but with certain substitutes in place of colours, see Fig. 1.

Fig. 1. Key for Chart Symbols

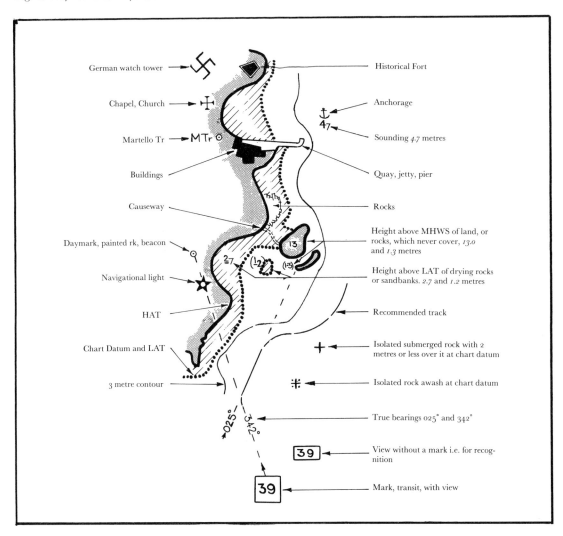

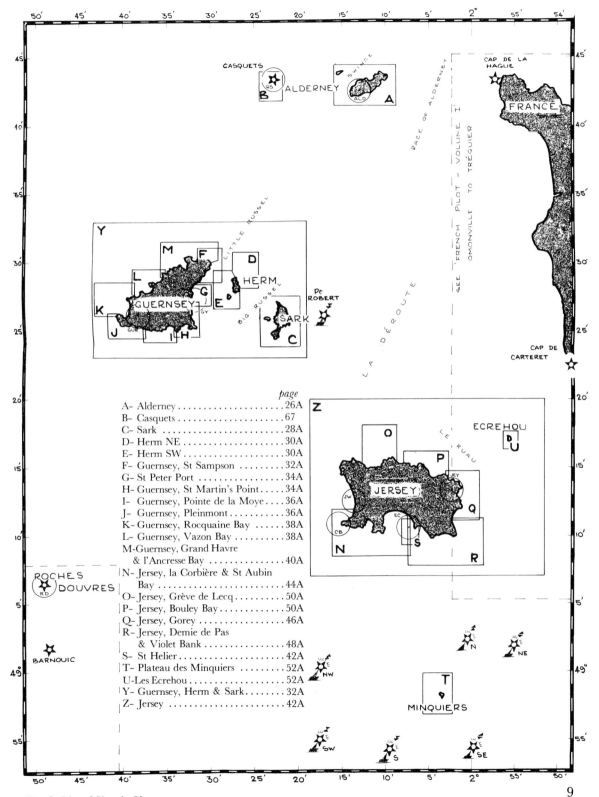

Fig. 2. List of Sketch Charts

9

The symbol for rocks is seldom shown – most of the Channel Island dangers are rocks anyway – which means that an area shown as drying may consist of rocks, sand, mud, shingle, or a combination of the lot. The quality of the bottom has been left out; however no anchorages are indicated in poor holding ground.

Compass roses are omitted, the chart margin is true north. The E or W margin shows minutes of latitude and tenths, i.e. nautical miles and cables. The S margin is in minutes and tenths of longitude. One ca. = 185m = 608ft. Form lines on the land are in metres at 25m intervals, with occasional spot heights, all measured above MHWS.

The shape, colour, top-mark and light character of buoys follow Admiralty symbol chart 5011 – but the purple flash has had to be replaced by a rather clumsy light star. The buoys are listed on p. 10. Jersey and Minquiers buoys have their names prefixed by the word JERSEY; they are supplied and maintained by the States, Guernsey and Sark by Trinity House.

My sketch charts are not a substitute for Admiralty charts; they – and any of the following publications – can be bought from official chart agents – i.e. South Pier Shipyard, St Helier, Jersey, Boatworks+ and Navigation & Marine Supplies, St Peter Port, Guernsey.

Catalogue of charts, Home edition	NP 109
Tidal Stream Atlas	NP 264
List of Radio Signals Vol 2	NP 282
Tide Tables Vol I	NP 201
The Mariner's Handbook	NP 100
List of Lights, Vol. A	NP 74
Channel Pilot	NP 27
Symbols & Abbreviations	Chart 5011

The transits shown on the charts are drawn in solid line for the working part. It may be extended at either end, toward or away from marks; it is then a pecked line. Lines with long dashes are recommended tracks; either these don't require a set of marks, or there are no objects available to use as a transit. Every transit is sketched in elevation – same number as on the chart. Fig. 3 shows an imaginary typical transit. In the text the rear mark is given first, followed by the front mark. In Fig. 3 the text and caption might read '90: So-and-so Tower × such-and-such Beacon' (× is used instead of 'by'). If, as sometimes happens, the front mark obscures the rear, then I have drawn the marks slightly offset for clarity. If this slight deviation is permissible, no mention is made in the text.

Marks offset to one side or the other are called 'Opened'. In Fig. 3 the 2 towers, line 90, are exactly in transit on bearing 137°. However, if the marks had to be 'opened to the right', then the rear tower would have to be seen slightly to the right of the front tower. The correct amount to open each mark is shown on every view; here are some examples:

Line 36 – The German tower is opened by 2 breadths of a building, Fort Corblets.
Line 261 – Noirmont is not central in the gap by a proportion given.
Line 266 – Here are three rocks. The span (S) between two is $2\frac{1}{2}$ times the other two.

In Fig. 3 there is also a separate view of the rear mark, since it is small and far away. The view 89, is in a rectangle. If it is helpful to give the state of tide in a view, it is shown in the bottom right hand corner. Needless to say my pictures are not to scale and often the perspective has been fiddled for clarity.

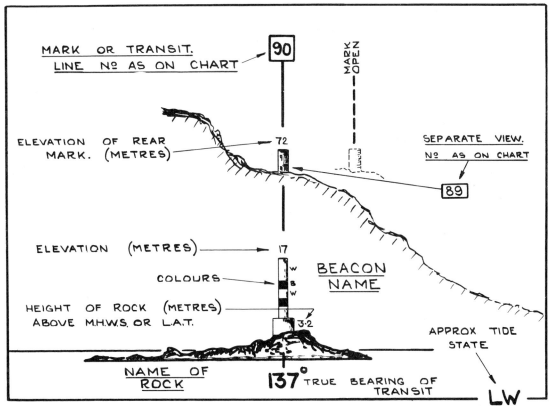

Fig. 3. Typical view

Just a re-cap on the line numbers in views and on charts. Both are the same number ...

Within a SQUARE   – Transit on a chart and in a view.
Within a RECTANGLE – Separate view of a buoy, beacon, rock, drawn large for recognition.

When changing from one transit to another when the course alteration is small, a breast mark is sometimes helpful. For example in the Gument Passage, Jersey, line 263 is a breast mark. It tells you when to quit line 262 and take line 264.

Depth in channels is nearly always shown in brackets after the title. e.g. the minimum depth in the Tobar Passage, p. 82, is, when keeping on the transits, 5.0m.

This is a book about pilotage marks. It is not a text on general navigation, nor do I tell you about obvious chart features, early closing days or bad restaurants.

List of Channel Island Buoys

Name	Location N	W	IALA Mark	Light	Sound
Jersey					
Baleine	49°10·5′	2°08·1′	Stb'd		
Canger Rock	49°07·4′	2°00·3′	Card W	QkFl(9).15s	
Cochon	49°09·9′	1°58·7′	Port		
Demie de Frèmont	49°15·6′	2°07·3′	Stb'd		
Desormes	49°19·0′	2°17·9′	Card W	VQkFl(9).15s	
Diamond	49°10·1′	2°08·6′	Port	Gp(2)R.6s	
East Rock	49°10·0′	2°07·2′	Stb'd	QkFlG	
Ecrivière	49°15·3′	1°52·2′	Card S	VQkFl(6)+LFl.15s	Bell
Les Fours	49°09·7′	2°10·1′	Card N	VQkFl	
Giffard	49°10·7′	1°58·9′	Port		
Gorey Roads	49°11·5′	2°00·2′	Stb'd	QkFlG April–October	
Grunes du Port	49°10·1′	2°09·0′	Port		
Hinguette	49°09·4′	2°07·2′	Port	Gp(4)R.15s	
Passage Rock	49°09·6′	2°12·2′	Card N	VQkFl	
Ruaudière	49°09·8′	2°08·5′	Stb'd	FlG.3s	Bell
Sillette	49°09·2′	2°09·4′	Port		
Violet Channel	49°07·9′	1°57·1′	Safe water	LFl.10s	
Frouquier Aubert	49°06·2′	1°58·8′	Card S	VQkFl(6) + LFl.15s	
Minquiers					
Demie de Vascelin	49°00·9′	2°05·1′	Stb'd		
N Minquiers	49°01·7′	2°00·5′	Card N	QkFl	
NE Minquiers	49°00·9′	1°55·2′	Card E	VQkFl(3).5s	Bell
SE Minquiers	48°53·5′	2°00·0′	Card E	QkFl(3).10s	Bell
S Minquiers	48°53·1′	2°10·1′	Card S	QkFl(6)+LFl.15s	
SW Minquiers	48°54·4′	2°19·3′	Card W	VQkFl(9).15s	Whistle
NW Minquiers	48°59·7′	2°20·5′	Card N	VQkFl	Bell
Guernsey and Sark					
Blanchard	49°25·4′	2°17·3′	Card E	VQkFl(3).10s	Whistle
Lower Heads	49°25·9′	2°28·6′	Card S	VQkFl(6)+LFl.15s	Bell
Petite Canupe	49°30·2′	2°29·0′	Card S		
Reffée	49°27.8′	2°31.2′	Card S	VQkFl(6) + LFl.10s	
Fourquies Rock	49°27.3′	2°26.5′	Card N	VQkFl	

Radio Beacons

These are shown on charts as a circle with the identification letters inside. All are continuous – see Fig. 2. For details of adjacent radio beacons, see Admiralty list of Radio Signals – Vol 2.

Name	Type	Ident	Frequency kHz	Emission	Range miles	Position N	W
Casquets (c)	RC	QS	298.8	A2	50	49°43·4′	2°22·5′
Roches Douvres (c)	RC	RD			70	49°06·5′	2°49·1′
Alderney	Aero RC	ALD	383	Ao,A2	50	49°42·6′	2°11·9′
Guernsey	Aero RC	GUR	361	Ao,A2	30	49°26·1′	2°38·3′
Jersey East	Aero RC	JEY	367	Ao,A2	75	49°13·2′	2°02·1′
Jersey West	Aero RC	JW	329	Ao,A2	25	49°12·4′	2°13·3′
St Helier Harbour	RC	EC	287·3	A2	10	49°10·6′	2°07·5′
Corbière (a)	RC	CB	305·7	A2	20	49°10·8′	2°14·9′
Castle Breakwater, St Peter Port (b)	RC	GY	285	A2	10	49°27·3′	2°31·3′

(a) Corbière. Grouped with Cap Fréhel.
Corbière transmits in sequence 2, 4 and 6 (i.e. minutes) past the hour 00–01 Cap Fréhel, 01–02 Corbière, 02–03 Cap Fréhel, 03–04 Corbière, 04–05 Cap Fréhel, 05–06 Corbière, etc. as follows:

In clear weather			**In poor visibility**		
CB 4 times	24 secs.	500Hz	CB 4 times	24 secs.	500Hz
Long dash	25 secs.	500Hz	Long dash	18 secs.	500Hz
CB once	6 secs.	500Hz	13 pips	13 secs.	1,000Hz
Silence period	5 secs.		Silent period	5 secs.	
Total	60 secs.		Total	60 secs.	

The commencement of the Lighthouse Fog Signal Horn Morse (C) is coincident with the end of the 18 seconds long dash of the Radio Beacon code. Each 1,000Hz 'pip' heard on the Radio Beacon code before hearing the commencement of the Fog Signal represents a distance off the Lighthouse of approximately 335 metres. Several observations are recommended.

(b) Castle Breakwater Lt, St Peter Port. Synchronized with a horn for distance finding. The blast of the horn begins simultaneously with the 27-second long dash after the four GY identification signals. The number of seconds from the start of the long dash until the horn blast is heard, when multiplied by the factor 0·18, corresponds to the distance from the horn in nautical miles.

(c) Grouped in the following sequence with other beacons at 1-minute intervals:

1	Penlee Point	PE
2	Start Point	SP
3	Casquets	QS
4	Roches Douvres	RD
5	Ile Vierge	VG
6	Lizard	LZ

Channel Islands Pilot

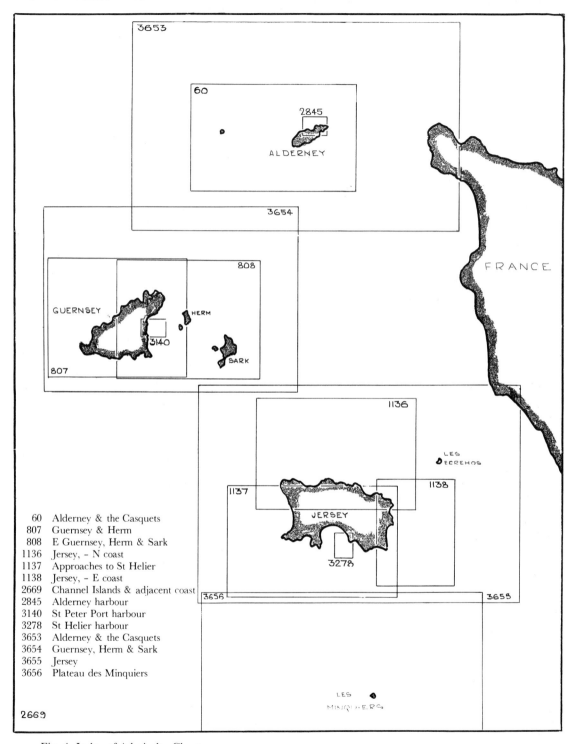

60   Alderney & the Casquets
807 Guernsey & Herm
808 E Guernsey, Herm & Sark
1136 Jersey, – N coast
1137 Approaches to St Helier
1138 Jersey, – E coast
2669 Channel Islands & adjacent coast
2845 Alderney harbour
3140 St Peter Port harbour
3278 St Helier harbour
3653 Alderney & the Casquets
3654 Guernsey, Herm & Sark
3655 Jersey
3656 Plateau des Minquiers

Fig. 4. Index of Admiralty Charts

14

Marks and Transit Lines

Glossary

About	E.g. S-about is to set a course to leave an object to the north
Aiguille	Needle
Amont	Upstream in a tidal current, landward, easternmost
Aval	Downstream in a tidal current, seaward
Bas, -se	Low rock
Boue	Rock mostly submerged
Col	Neck
Crossroads	Where two or more marks meet
Demi-e	Half-tide rock
Dog-leg	Two courses parallel but offset
Fosse	Ditch, channel
Gateway	Course between two objects
Goulet	Narrow entrance
Grand, -e	Big
Grève	Sandy beach
Grune	Rock, not always submerged
Handrail	Passing around an object, or several, on the one hand
Havre	Haven
Mare	Tide
Moie	High Rock
Moulin	Mill
Nez	Nose
Noir, -e	Black, dark
Nord	North
Petit, -e	Small
Pierre	Stone
Pignon	Gable
Platte	Level, flat
Pointe	Point
Pont	Bridge
Port	Harbour, inlet
Raz	Swift tidal stream
Rousse	Reddish
Sud	South
Tête	Head
Town	Usual name for St Peter Port or St Helier
Val	Narrow valley
×	In line with, by

Tides

Tides don't invariably follow the prognostications printed out by tide-table computers. Nowhere is this more obvious than in the Channel Islands – a high barometer, for example, will lower the water level by ⅓m for every 30 millibars. By itself this isn't too great; but what about the sound effects? Like a prolonged wind from one quarter, a storm surge, a seiche – then the tabulated heights and times make nonsense.

The diagram, Fig. 5 shows, relative to a common horizontal half-tide line, the tidal heights of the 4 islands. It also illustrates how the ranges and times vary with distance from St Helier. The convenience of this half-tide line or level has been explained elsewhere. The same information is tabulated in Fig. 6.

12 hourly tidal stream charts, showing rate and direction, with reference to St Helier, are printed inside the front and back covers of this pilot. They are numbered 1–12, commencing at half-tide down, St Helier. They show the average conditions, not on the hour of each chart exactly, but roughly during a period plus and minus half an hour. The 12 tidal charts are diagrammatic only – they are not to scale. All times are those of the Channel Islands standard port, St Helier. The streams are in tenths of knots – the greater value at springs, the lesser neaps.

Another useful value is given on each hourly chart. Against each island is a square containing two values; the upper figure is the rise at springs, the lower is the rise at neaps, both at the hour of each chart. The rise is from the chart datum, measured in metres (decimal tenths). To reduce possibility of error further, there is a small *aide memoire* in a square at the top-left corner of each hourly chart: S(prings) are on top. N(eaps) at the bottom. Mental interpolation is simple merely by inspection of adjacent hour charts. How about some examples?

(1) HW St Helier, my tide-table tells me, will be at 2305 tonight, height 8·0m. At what time will I have a 3m rise in Alderney? Chart HW tells me that this 8.0m rise is almost dead neaps. Turn back the charts while looking at the lower (neap) value in Alderney's square. Chart 4 (LW) shows only a 2·4m rise – too small. Chart 5 shows 2·5m – still too low. Chart 6 – nearly enough at 2·9m. But Chart 7 says we shall have 3·4m at half-tide up – i.e. 3 hours before HW at Helier, or about 2000 hrs.

(2) I am approaching Grand Havre, hoping to be able to get alongside the quay. My boat draws 4 ft. My ETA will be about 1515 – can I do this? First the tide tables: St Helier HW was at 1117 today, height 8·4m. Inspection of the tide tables also tells me that I am only 2 days off neaps. If HW was at 1117, then my ETA of 1515 is 4 hours later. I then look at Chart 2 (HW + 4) and see in the Guernsey square that the rise will be 3·7m at springs and 4·5 at neaps. Today is 2 days, about a third, between neaps and springs say (mental interpolation) 4·2m. Now I learn from p. 105 that Grand Havre quay dries _2.3m,_ so the depth at about 1515 will be 1.9m or 5ft 9in (4.2 – 2.3 = 1.9m). Just nice time. The difference in rise around the coast of each island isn't worth bothering about, and for Herm use Guernsey figures.

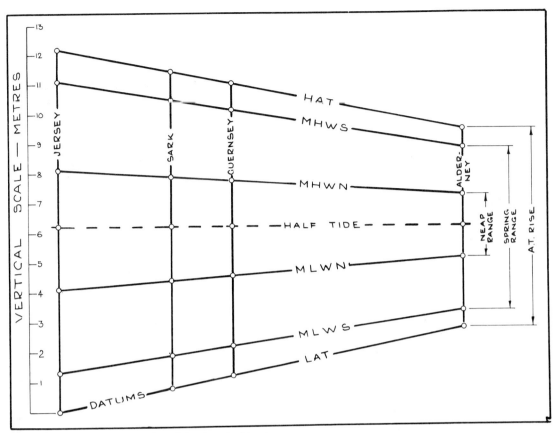

Fig. 5. Diagram of tidal heights of the 4 main islands

			Heights					Ranges		Time diff. from St Helier minutes	
		Astronomical tides		Mean Springs		Mean Neaps		Mean half tide	Mean springs	Mean neaps		
		HAT	LAT	MHWS	MLWS	MHWN	MLWN	HT			springs	neaps
Column		1	2	3	4	5	6	7	8	9	10	11
Jersey St Helier		12·2	NIL	11·1	1·3	8·1	4·1	6·2	9·8	4·0	NIL	NIL
Sark Creux Hr		10·6	NIL	9·7	1·1	7·1	3·6	5·4	8·6	3·5	+10	+5
Guernsey St Peter Port		9·8	NIL	8·9	1·0	6·6	3·4	5·0	7·9	3·2	+10	+0
Alderney Braye Hr		6·7	NIL	6·1	0·6	4·5	2·4	3·4	5·5	2·1	+35	+50

Fig. 6. Tabulated tidal data for the 4 main islands.

Just a reminder or so . . . BST or GMT (but not both) . . . use St Helier times for the tidal charts . . . are you on a rising or a falling tide? The figures for half-tide up and half-tide down aren't quite the same.

The tide tables for, and nearly all the Admiralty charts on, the Channel Islands have been reduced to a new datum since about 1964. This datum, used in this book, is LAT. For Figs. 5 and 6, the definitions are explained below. Column Nos refer to Fig. 6.

HAT (Highest astronomical tide) **LAT** (Lowest astronomical tide) cols 1 and 2, are the levels which can be predicted to occur under average meteorological conditions and under any combination of astronomical movements.

MHWS (Mean high-water springs) **MLWS** (Mean low-water springs) cols 3 and 4, are the average rises throughout the year on two successive tides when the moon is at $23\frac{1}{2}°$ declination and the tide is greatest.

MHWN (Mean high-water neaps) **MLWN** (Mean low-water neaps), cols 5 and 6, are for the same conditions in cols. 3 and 4 but when the tide is least.

HT (Mean half-tide) col 7, is a convenient level peculiar to the big tidal ranges of the Channel Islands. It is the average of 4 figures; the rise at half-tide up, half-tide down, at springs and at neaps.

RANGES, cols 8 and 9, are arithmetical. Col 3 – col 4 = col 8. Col 5 – col 6 = col 9.

TIME differences, cols 10 and 11 are the minutes after St Helier of tide times on other islands. Dover is about $4\frac{3}{4}$ hours AFTER St Helier.

The leading tidal definitions are on the sectional diagram in Fig. 8. Throughout the text an underlined figure in italics (e.g. *1·2m*) gives the height in metres which a rock dries out about LAT (Chart Datum).

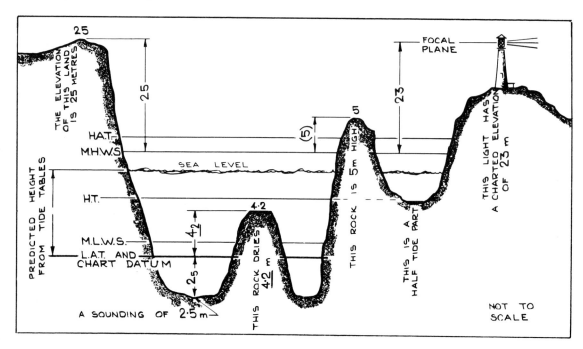

Fig. 8. Tidal definitions

20

CHANNEL ISLANDS YACHT MARINA (BEAUCETTE)
DEPTH OVER SILL IN METRES (SILL DRIES 2m 37)

Predicted Height of H.W. at St. Peter Port	H.W.	±1 hr	±2 hrs	±2½ hrs	Half Tide ±3 hrs	±3½ hrs	±4 hrs	±5 hrs	±6 hrs (L.W.)
6.00	3.65	3.50	3.20	2.98	2.75	2.52	2.30	2.00	1.85
.20	3.85	3.67	3.30	3.03	..	2.47	2.20	1.83	1.65
.40	4.05	3.84	3.40	3.08	..	2.42	2.10	1.66	1.45
.60	4.25	4.00	3.50	3.13	..	2.37	2.00	1.52	1.25
.80	4.45	4.17	3.60	3.18	..	2.32	1.90	1.33	1.05
7.00	4.65	4.34	3.70	3.23	..	2.27	1.80	1.16	.85
.20	4.85	4.50	3.80	3.28	..	2.22	1.70	1.00	.65
.40	5.05	4.67	3.90	3.33	..	2.17	1.60	.83	.45
.60	5.25	4.84	4.00	3.38	..	2.12	1.50	.66	.25
.80	5.45	5.00	4.10	3.43	..	2.07	1.40	.50	.05
8.00	5.65	5.17	4.20	3.48	..	2.02	1.30	.33	—
.20	5.85	5.34	4.30	3.53	..	1.97	1.20	.16	—
.40	6.05	5.50	4.40	3.58	..	1.92	1.10	—	—
.60	6.25	5.67	4.50	3.63	..	1.87	1.00	—	—
.80	6.45	5.84	4.60	3.68	..	1.82	.90	—	—
9.00	6.65	6.00	4.70	3.73	..	1.77	.80	—	—
.20	6.85	6.17	4.80	3.78	..	1.72	.70	—	—
.40	7.05	6.34	4.90	3.83	..	1.67	.60	—	—
.60	7.25	6.50	5.00	3.88	..	1.62	.50	—	—
.80	7.45	6.67	5.10	3.93	..	1.57	.40	—	—
10.00	7.65	6.84	5.20	3.98	..	1.52	.30	—	—

VICTORIA MARINA
DEPTH OVER SILL IN METRES (SILL DRIES 4m 10)

Predicted Height of H.W. at St Peter Port	H.W.	±1 hr	±2 hr	±2½ hrs	Half Tide ±3 hrs	±3½ hrs	±4 hrs	±5 hrs	±6 hrs (L.W.)
6.00	1.75	1.60	1.30	1.08	.85	.62	.40	.10	—
.20	1.95	1.77	1.40	1.13	..	.57	.30	—	—
.40	2.15	1.94	1.50	1.18	..	.52	.20	—	—
.60	2.35	2.10	1.60	1.23	..	.47	.10	—	—
.80	2.55	2.27	1.70	1.28	..	.42	—	—	—
7.00	2.75	2.44	1.80	1.33	..	.37	—	—	—
.20	2.95	2.60	1.90	1.38	..	.32	—	—	—
.40	3.15	2.77	2.00	1.43	..	.27	—	—	—
.60	3.35	2.94	2.10	1.48	..	.22	—	—	—
.80	3.55	3.10	2.20	1.53	..	.17	—	—	—
8.00	3.75	3.27	2.30	1.58	..	.12	—	—	—
.20	3.95	3.44	2.40	1.63	..	.07	—	—	—
.40	4.15	3.60	2.50	1.68	..	.02	—	—	—
.60	4.35	3.77	2.60	1.73	..	—	—	—	—
.80	4.55	3.94	2.70	1.78	..	—	—	—	—
9.00	4.75	4.10	2.80	1.83	..	—	—	—	—
.20	4.95	4.27	2.90	1.88	..	—	—	—	—
.40	5.15	4.44	3.00	1.93	..	—	—	—	—
.60	5.35	4.60	3.10	1.98	..	—	—	—	—
.80	5.55	4.77	3.20	2.03	..	—	—	—	—
10.00	5.75	4.94	3.30	2.08	..	—	—	—	—

ALBERT MARINA
DEPTH OVER SILL IN METRES (SILL DRIES 3m 80)

Predicted Height of H W at St Peter Port	H W	±1 hr	±2 hrs	±2½ hrs	Half Tide ±3 hrs	±3½ hrs	±4 hrs	±5 hrs	±6 hrs (L W)
6.00	2.15	2.00	1.70	1.48	1.25	1.02	.80	.50	.35
.20	2.35	2.17	1.80	1.53	..	.97	.70	.33	.15
.40	2.55	2.34	1.90	1.58	..	.92	.60	.16	—
.60	2.75	2.50	2.00	1.63	..	.87	.50	.02	—
.80	2.95	2.67	2.10	1.68	..	.82	.40	—	—
7.00	3.15	2.84	2.20	1.73	..	.77	.30	—	—
.20	3.35	3.00	2.30	1.78	..	.72	.20	—	—
.40	3.55	3.17	2.40	1.83	..	.67	.10	—	—
.60	3.75	3.34	2.50	1.88	..	.62	—	—	—
.80	3.95	3.50	2.60	1.93	..	.57	—	—	—
8.00	4.15	3.67	2.70	1.98	..	.52	—	—	—
.20	4.35	3.84	2.80	2.03	..	.47	—	—	—
.40	4.55	4.00	2.90	2.08	..	.42	—	—	2.0
.60	4.75	4.17	3.00	2.13	..	.37	—	—	—
.80	4.95	4.34	3.10	2.18	..	.32	—	—	—
9.00	5.15	4.50	3.20	2.23	..	.27	—	—	—
.20	5.35	4.67	3.30	2.28	..	.22	—	—	—
.40	5.55	4.84	3.40	2.33	..	.17	—	—	—
.60	5.75	5.00	3.50	2.38	..	.12	—	—	—
.80	5.95	5.17	3.60	2.43	..	.07	—	—	—
10.00	6.15	5.34	3.70	2.48	..	.02	—	—	—

How to use these tables.

(a) From St Peter Port tide tables extract the predicted height and times of High Water. Enter the left-hand column with this height.

(b) From this height horizontally across the other columns are the depths of water over the sill in METRES.

Example: At 1530 it was HW St Peter Fort; height = 8·4m. What will the depth be on Beaucette Yacht Marina sill at 1900 on the same day? 1900 is 3½ hours after HW. With height 8·4m and on the same line, under column headed ±3½, there is the answer ...1·92m.

Local Information

Government. Though not completely true, visiting yachtsmen might do well to think of the Channel Islands as 4 separate governments. Headed by a Crown-appointed Governor and Bailiff, Jersey has its own legislature – the States of Jersey. Guernsey is the same, with the States of Guernsey, but its Bailiwick also includes Sark and Alderney. There is a President in Alderney and the States of Alderney have seats in the States of Guernsey. Sark is more independent – its government is the Chief Pleas – and more feudal; it has a Seigneur. Herm and Jethou are an integral part of Guernsey; Brecqhou is part of Sark; the Minquiers and les Ecrehou belong to Jersey.

All 4 islands have their own courts in which justice is dished out without delay, for example, to foolish yachtsmen who ignore the very few simple regulations.

Customs. International 'Q' flags are compulsory. Whether you come from another island or from outside you may only enter at the following harbours. You must complete crew lists and Customs declaration forms.

Jersey	– St Helier, Gorey.
Guernsey	– St Peter Port, St Sampson, Beaucette marina (as a concession).
Alderney	– Braye harbour.
Sark	– No specific regulations.

As a concession, however, you may clear outwards from any part of any island.

Immigration. There are no inter-island formalities. The same immigration regulations as in the UK apply to all the islands.

Except to and from the UK all crew must have passports and must complete immigration clearance. This applies whether they travel by yacht, join a yacht here or quit a yacht in the islands. There are Customs officers in Jersey, Guernsey, Sark and Alderney.

Duty-free stores are available for yachts above a certain size bound for a particular destination, details from:

Jersey	– Impôts Dept., Weighbridge, St Helier.
Guernsey	– Customs & Immigration, White Rock, St Peter Port.
Sark & Alderney	– Not available.

Medicine. All islands except Sark have reciprocal arrangements with the UK. There are hospitals in Guernsey, Jersey and Alderney – Sark has one doctor only.

Currency is sterling but Jersey and Guernsey issue their own money. All except coin are freely interchangeable with the UK.

Stamps. Guernsey Bailiwick stamps or Jersey stamps, respectively, must be used for outgoing mail. These islands operate their own post offices and telephone systems.

Rabies. Unless from the UK, Isle of Man or Eire, no animals whatsoever may be landed anywhere in the Channel Islands – and this means beaches, rocks, islets, quays. If you are caught don't expect any mercy. First you will get a thumping fine; your animal may be immediately destroyed; as an afterthought you might be offered 6 months' quarantine at staggering cost. If, however, you are not caught but your pet is shot by some local citizen, well – I have heard about this once or twice, but never about an appeal!

Fishing underwater has not escaped the attention of the laws; neither have fishing seasons. Harbourmasters will be helpful.

Speed limits are in force in many bays, as are restrictions on water-skiing. Inside harbours the maximum speed in Jersey is 5 knots; in Guernsey and Alderney, 4 knots.

Safety

Unlike the UK, there are no coastguards in the islands. RNLI lifeboats are stationed at Alderney, St Helier and St Peter Port; French ones at St Malo, Granville and Cap de la Hague. Storm warnings are displayed at Fort Regent and St Helier.

Radio stations and Frequencies

Station name	Continuous watch	Office watch hours	Working	Recorded Weather tel. No.
Jersey Radio	2182 kHz Chan 16	2381 kHz Chan 16	1726 kHz 2104 kHz 2534 kHz Chan 82 Chan 25 Chan 14*	Jersey 185
St Peter Port Radio	2182 kHz Chan 16	2381 kHz Chan 16	1792 kHz 1810 kHz Chan 67 Chan 78 Chan 12*	Guernsey 64033
St Sampson's Harbour			Chan 12**	
Beaucette Marina		Chan 37 (M)	Chan 37 (M)	
Alderney Radio		Chan 16	Chan 12*	

Office hours are Monday – Friday, 0900–1700 local time.
*Port movements. **half-tide up to half-tide down.

Jersey coded wind information at la Corbière radiobeacon Frequency 305·7 kHz

Wind direction, force and maximum gust is transmitted automatically every 6 minutes – i.e. during minutes 05–06, etc., 11–12, etc. past the hour as follows:-

1 Call sign CB 4 times as normal, followed by –
2 A series of from 1–8 short dashes at 1000Hz indicating the average wind direction and representing the 8 cardinal points, commencing with –
One dash = NE
Two dashes = E
Clockwise to 8 dashes = N
3 Followed by –
Up to 8 short dashes at 500Hz indicating average wind in Beaufort Scale (8 meaning Force 8 or more).
4 Followed by –
One or more short dashes at 1000Hz indicating maximum gust experienced above the average reading in (3) above.

Example
Three dashes at 1000Hz = SE
Followed by Five dashes at 500Hz = Force 5
Followed by One dash at 1000Hz = Gusting 6
This information will be automatically updated for transmission on the next 6-minute period.

Weather Forecasts

JERSEY RADIO broadcast CI area shipping forecasts at 0645, 0745, 1245, 1845 & 2245 GMT. Frequencies: VHF Ch 25 & 82 (After notice on 16) and 1726 kHz.

Crabby Harbour, Braye in Alderney – looking North East.

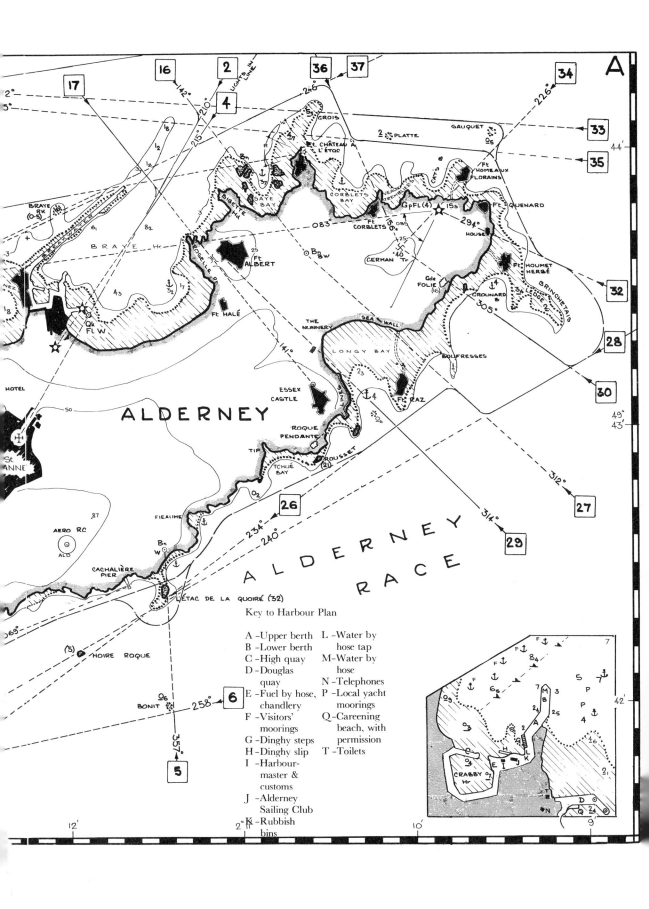

Key to Harbour Plan

A –Upper berth
B –Lower berth
C –High quay
D –Douglas quay
E –Fuel by hose, chandlery
F –Visitors' moorings
G –Dinghy steps
H –Dinghy slip
I –Harbour-master & customs
J –Alderney Sailing Club
K –Rubbish bins
L –Water by hose tap
M–Water by hose
N –Telephones
P –Local yacht moorings
Q –Careening beach, with permission
T –Toilets

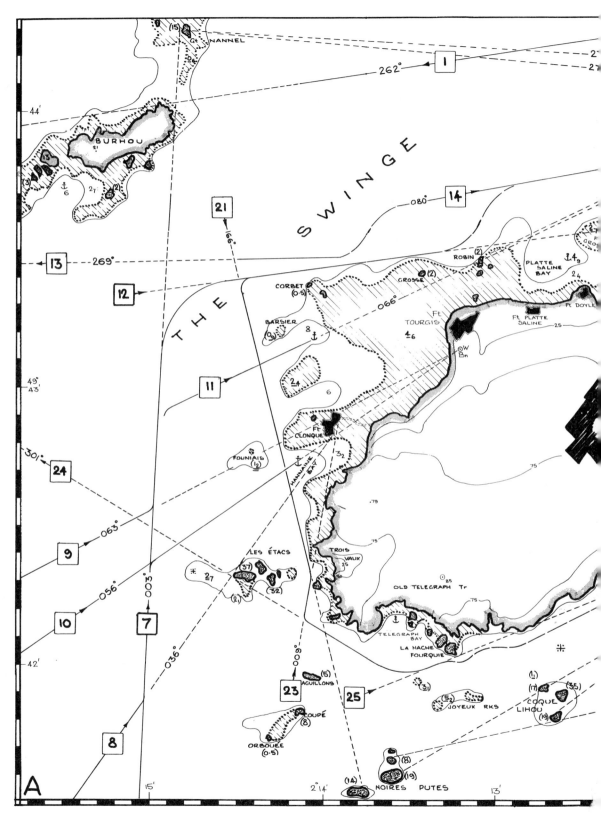

Chart A - Alderney

26A

Creux and Maseline Harbours in Sark.
Photo by Aerofilms

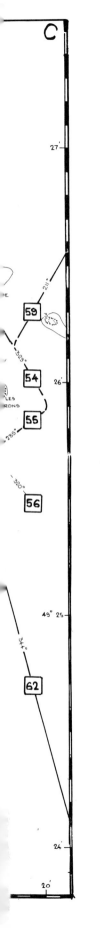

C

27'

211°

E

59

34°

329°

26'

LES
RONS

54

55

235°

300°

56

49° 25'

54°

62

24'

20'

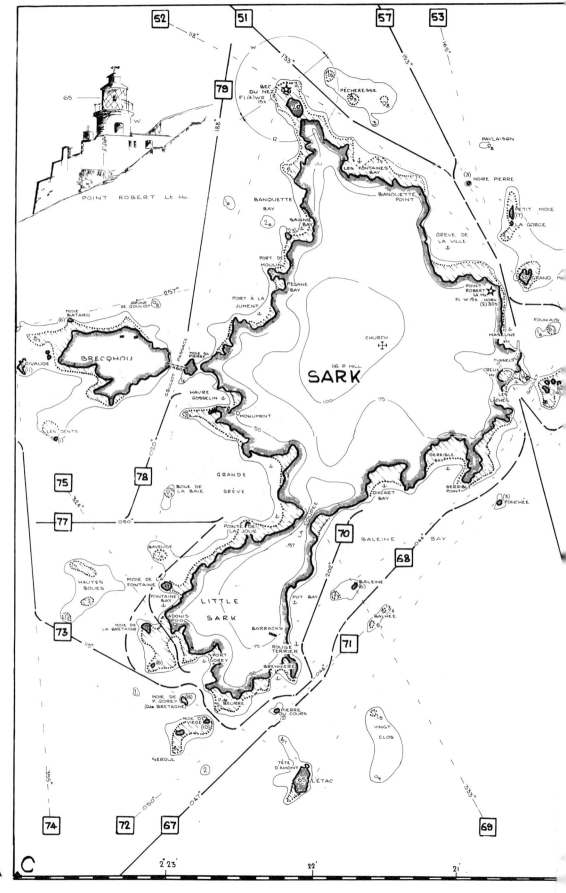

POINT ROBERT Lt Ho.

65

W

BREC DU NEZ
Fl (4) WR 15s

PÉCHERESSE

PAVLAISON

NOIRE PIERRE

PETIT MOIE
LA GORGE

LES FONTAINES
BAY

BANQUETTE
POINT

GRÈVE DE
LA VILLE

BANQUETTE
BAY

SAIGNIE
BAY

GRAND M

PORT DE
MOULIN

PEGANE
BAY

POINT
ROBERT Lt Ho
Fl W 15s HORN
(2) 30s

PORT À LA
JUMENT

FOUNIAIS

MOIE
BATARD

GRUNE
DE GOULIDT

CHURCH

MASELINE
Hr

SARK

TUNNELS

CREUX
Hr

LES LÂCHES

RIVAUDE

BRECQHOU

MOIE St
PIERRE

HAVRE
GOSSELIN

MONUMENT

LES DENTS

GRANDE

BOUE DE
LA BAIE

GRÈVE

DERRIBLE
BAY

DERRIBLE
POINT

CONCHÉE

POINTE DE
LA JOUE

LA COUPÉE

BALEINE   BAY

BAVEUSE

BALEINE

HAUTES
BOUES

MOIE DE LA
FONTAINE

LITTLE

POT BAY

BALMÉE

FONTAINE
BAY

ADONIS
POOL

SARK

MOIE DE
LA BRETAGNE

BARRACKS

ROUGE
TERRIER

PORT
GOREY

BRENNIÈRE

P. DE
BEURRE

MOIE DE
P. GOREY
(2de BRETAGNE)

PIERRE
DU COURS

MOIE DU
VIEDE

VINGT

CLOS

SERCUL

TÊTE
D'AMONT

L'ÉTAC

2° 23'   22'   21'

CHART C Sark

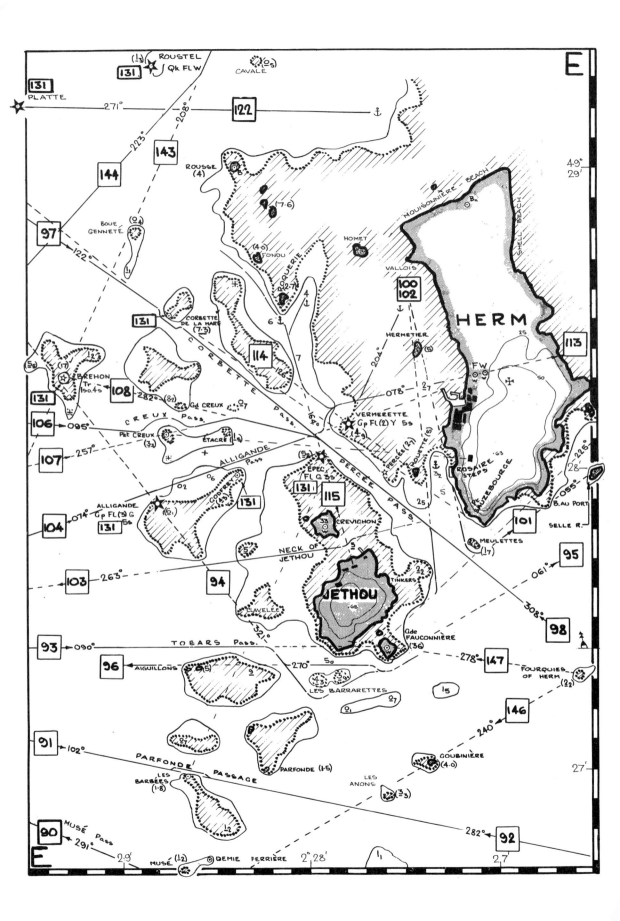

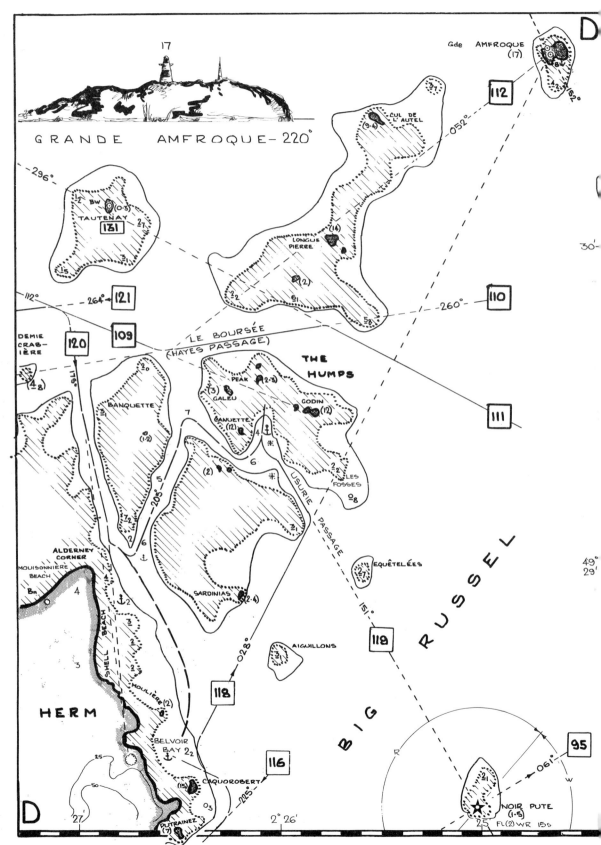

17

GRANDE AMFROQUE – 220°

Gde AMFROQUE (17)

112

052°

CUL DE L'AUTEL (9·4)

3·7

– 296°

BW (0·3)
TAUTENAY
131

2
27
4
3·1
1·5

(14)

LONGUE PIERRE

(2)

264° → 121

112°

109

110

260°

2·2
6·1
5·8

LE BOURSÉE
(HAYES PASSAGE)

DEMIE CRAB- IÈRE

120

115°

(4·8)

THE HUMPS

PEAK
(2·3)

(3) GALEU

GODIN (12)

2·0

BANQUETTE

19

7

BANQUETTE (12)

4

⚓

❋

111

(1·2)

(2)

6

❋

2·2 LES FOSSES

⁰8

205°

5

7·2

2

USURIE PASSAGE

3·1

ALDERNEY CORNER

⚓

6

EQUÊTELÉES (·7)

BIG

49° 29′

MOUISONNIÈRE BEACH

Bn
4

⚓
2

SARDINIAS (2·4)

RUSSEL

4

3

SHELL BEACH

2

3

028°

AIGUILLONS (·3)

119

151°

3

MOULIÈRE (2)

118

HERM

BELVOIR BAY 2·2
⚓

116

95

R

25

50

(15)

CAQUOROBERT

225°

·3

NOIR PUTE (1·5)

061°

W

D

27

2° 26′

PUTRAINEZ (7)

2·5 FL(2)WR 15s

30A

30′

30

Victoria Marina, St Peter Port, Guernsey

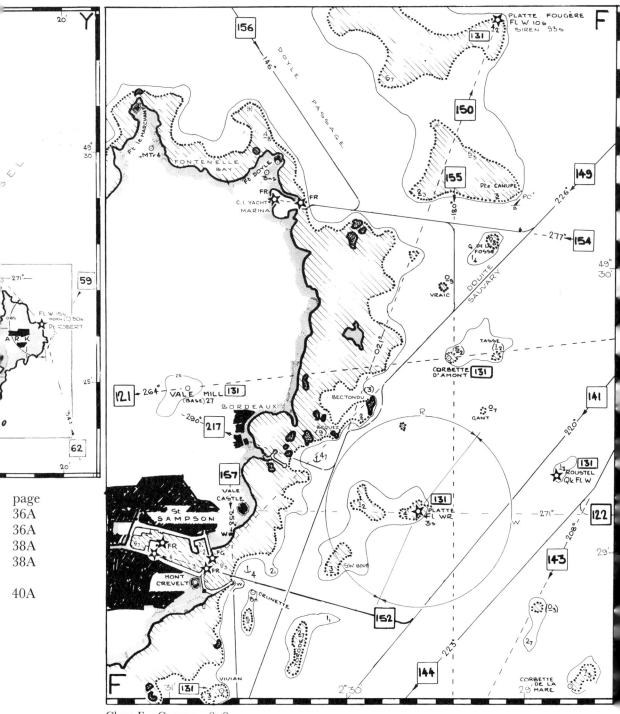

Chart F – Guernsey, St Sampson

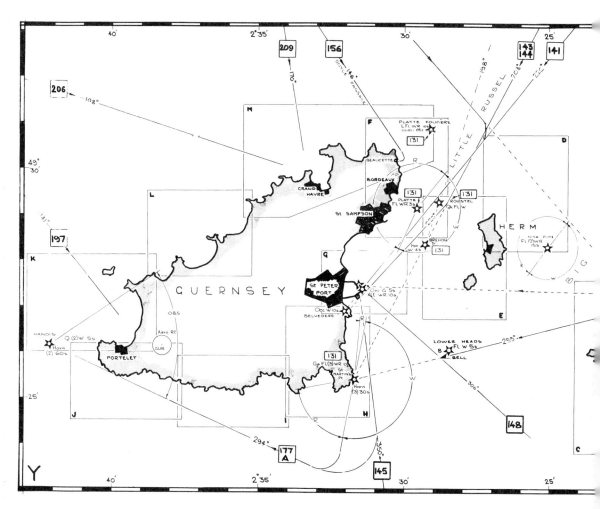

CHART Y Guernsey (with Herm and Sark)
CHART F Guernsey, St Sampson

Fermain Bay, Guernsey

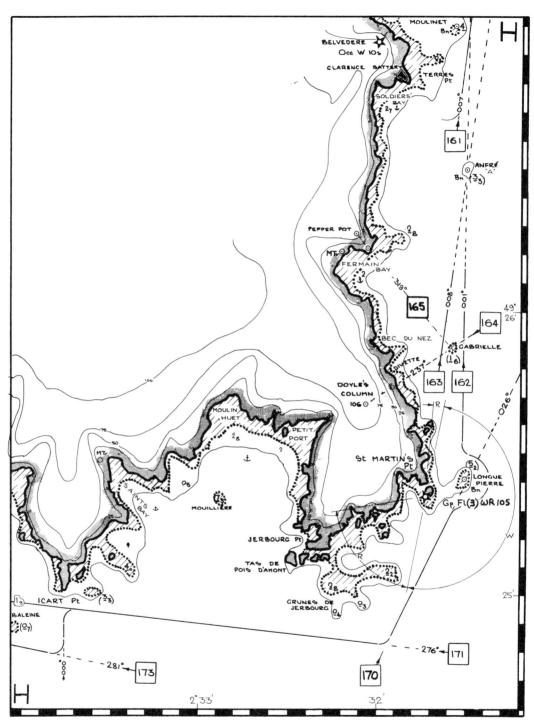

Chart H – Guernsey, St Martin's Point

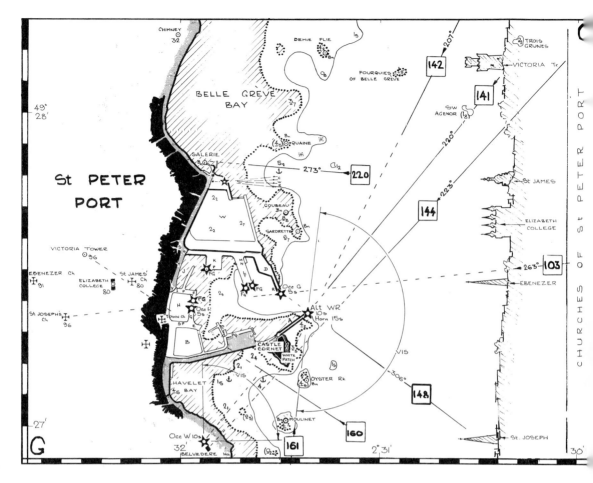

A – Castle breakwater
B – Albert dock marina, for local boats only
C – Patent slip 10 tons
D – White Rock Pier
E – Albert Pier
F – Victoria Pier
G – South Pier
H – Victoria marina, for local and visiting yachts
I – States of Guernsey Tourist Bureau
J – Careening hard, with Harbourmaster's permission
K – Cambridge berth
L – New jetty
M – Harbour office
N – Customs and Immigration
P – Water tap
Q – Fuel by hose
R – Port Signal station
S – Taxi rank
T – Telephone
U – Guernsey YC
V – Royal Channel Islands YC
W – North Beach marina, for local boats only

CHART G Guernsey, St Peter Port
CHART H Guernsey, St Martin's Point

Overlooking St Peter Port, Guernsey, with Sark in the far background.

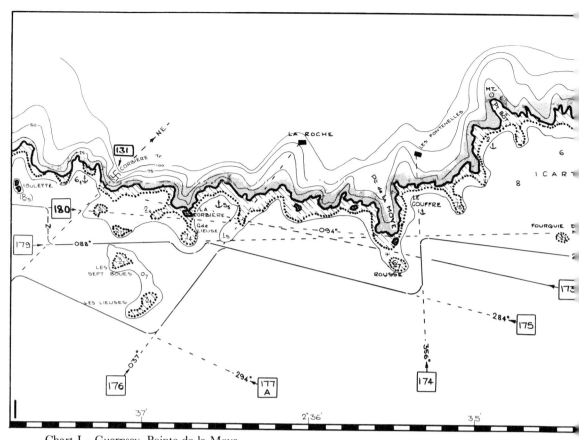

Chart I – Guernsey, Pointe de la Moye

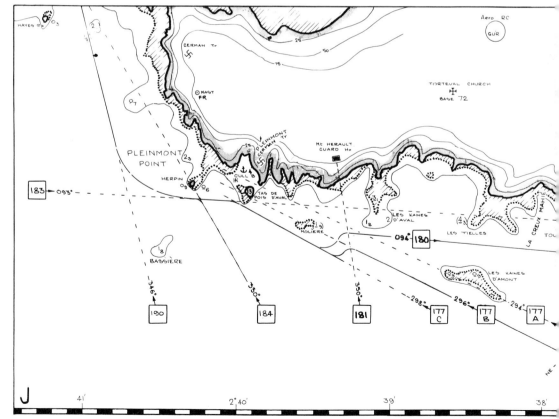

Chart J – Guernsey, Pleinmont

36A

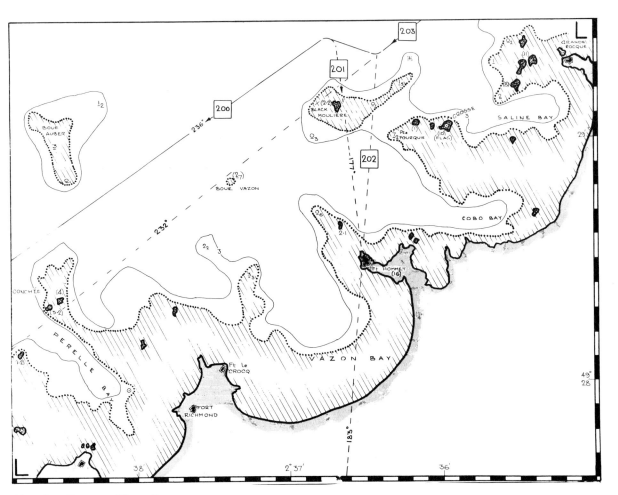

Chart L – Guernsey, Vazon Bay

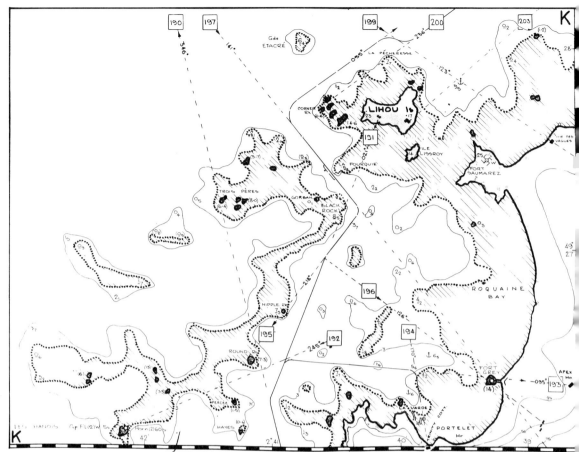

Chart K – Guernsey, Rocquaine Bay

CHART K Guernsey, Rocquaine Bay
CHART L Guernsey, Vazon Bay

38

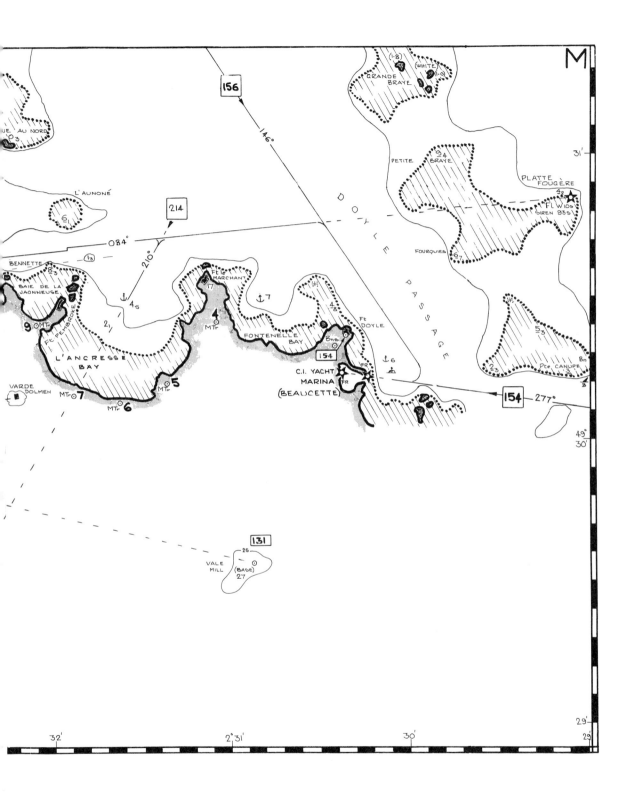

M

156

146°

31'

DOYLE

GRANDE BRAYE

(1.8)

(WHITE) 1.0

PETITE BRAYE 9.4

PLATTE FOUGÈRE
4.2
2

FL.W.10s
SIREN 93s

L'AUNONÉ

214

084°

6.1

210°

FOURQUIES 6.7

PASSAGE

BENNETTE

1.3

8.3

BAIE DE LA
JAONNEUSE

Ft
MARCHANT
7

5.3
5

Bn

2.3

Pte CANUPE
3

Ft PEMBROKE

9 O MTr

2.1

4.5

7

MTr

FONTENELLE
BAY

4.8

Ft
DOYLE

Bn
3

154

6

Bn
3

L'ANCRESSE
BAY

MTr

C.I. YACHT
MARINA
(BEAUCETTE)

FR

154 277°

VARDE
DOLMEN

MTr 7

MTr 5

MTr 6

FR

49'
30'

131

VALE
MILL

25

(BASE)
27

29'

32'

2°31'

30'

29

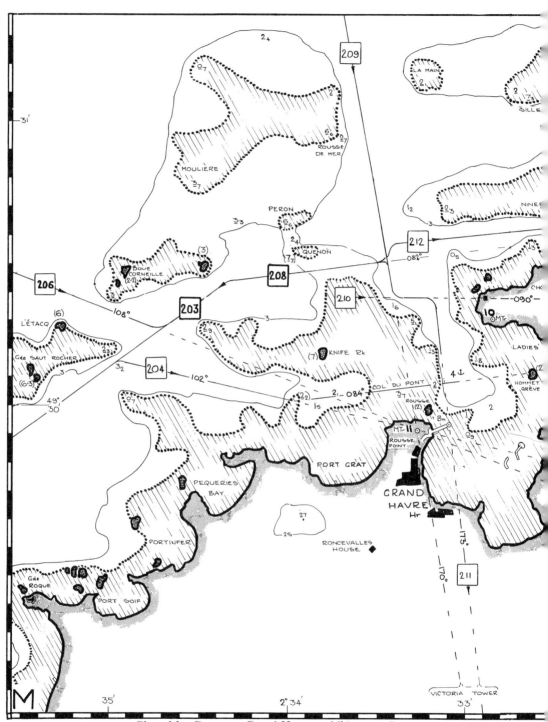

Chart M – Guernsey, Grand Havre and l'Ancresse Bay

40A

CHART M Guernsey, Grand Havre and L'Ancresse Bay

St Helier Marina, Jersey

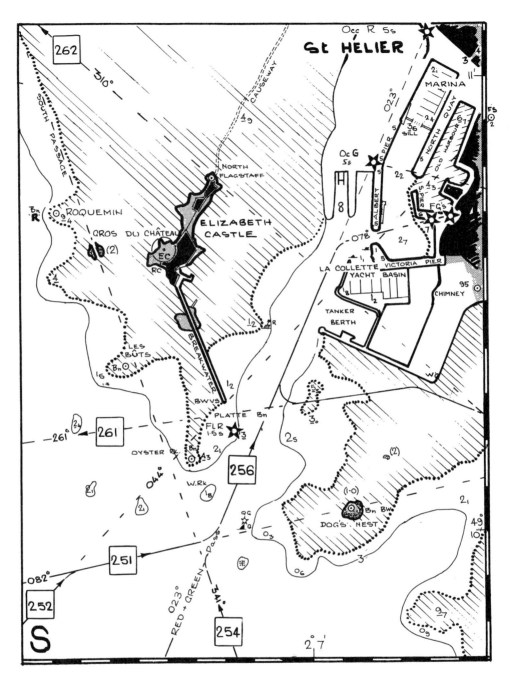

Chart S – St Helier and approaches

1 Signal station and port control
2 Signal mast, not used for port movements
3 Harbour Office
4 Customs, Immigration and States Tourist Bureau
5 Steamer berths
6 St Helier YC, fuel and water by hose
7 Dinghy slip
8 Ferry Terminal

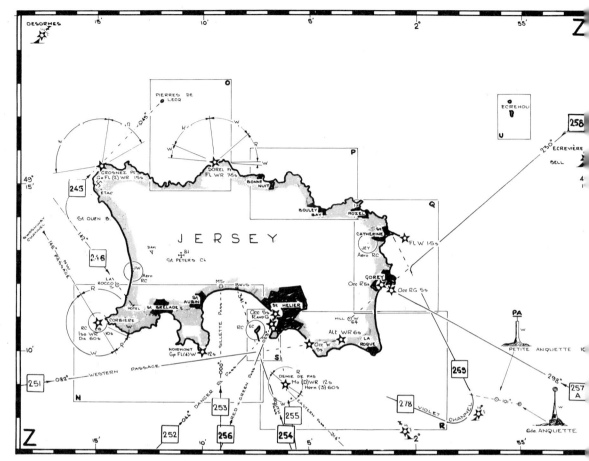

Chart Z - Jersey

N - Jersey, la Corbière &
    St Aubin Bay   44A
                              50A
O - Jersey, Grève de Lecq   50A
P - Jersey, Bouley Bay   46A
Q - Jersey, Gorey
R - Jersey, Demie de Pas &
    Violet Bank   48A
S - St Helier   42A
U - les Écrehou   52A

42A

CHART Z Jersey
CHART S Jersey, St Helier

St Aubin, Jersey

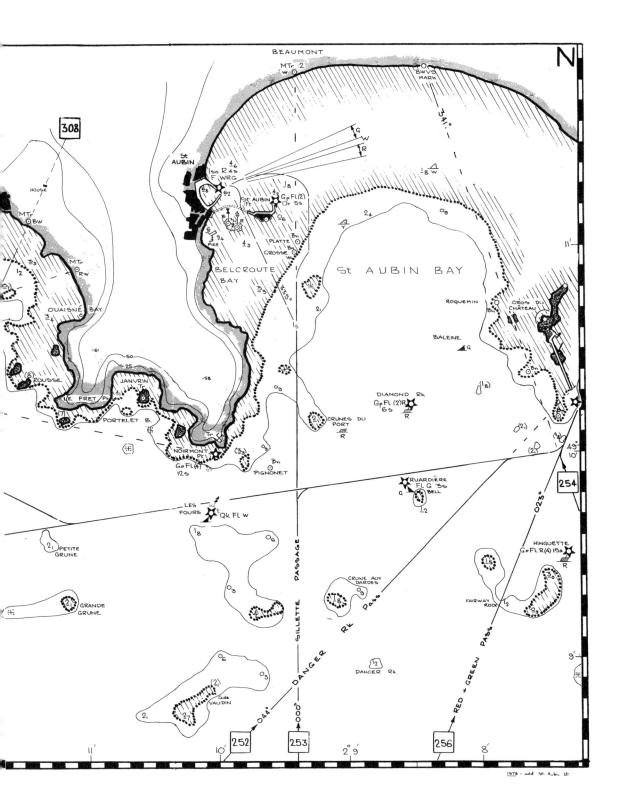

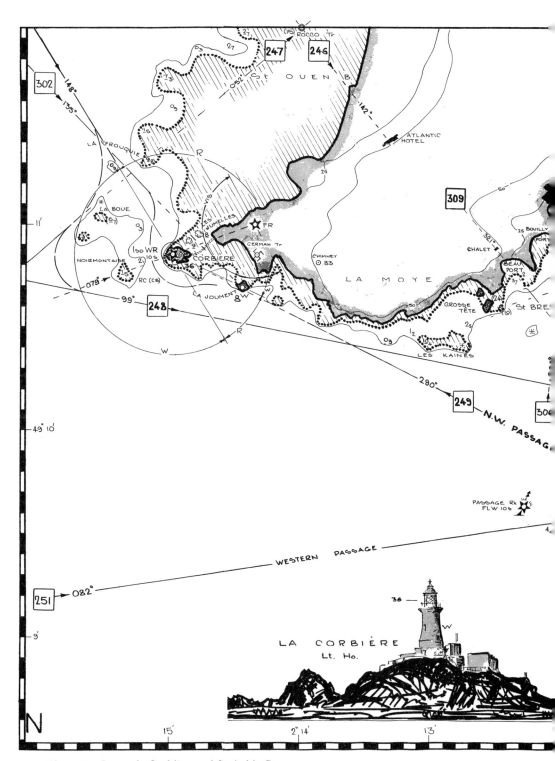

Chart N – Jersey, la Corbière and St Aubin Bay

44A

CHART N Jersey, la Corbière and St Aubin Bay

Mont Orgueil and Gorey Harbour, Jersey

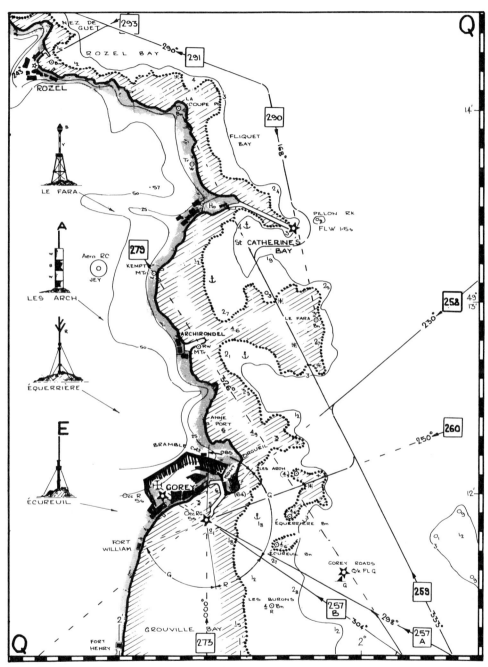

Chart Q – Jersey, Gorey

46A

CHART Q Jersey, Gorey

Rozel Harbour, Jersey

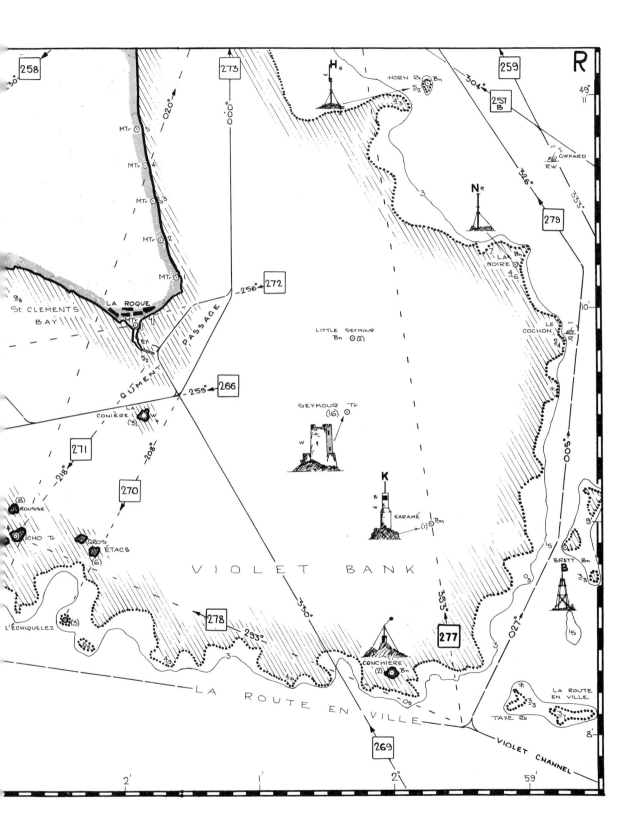

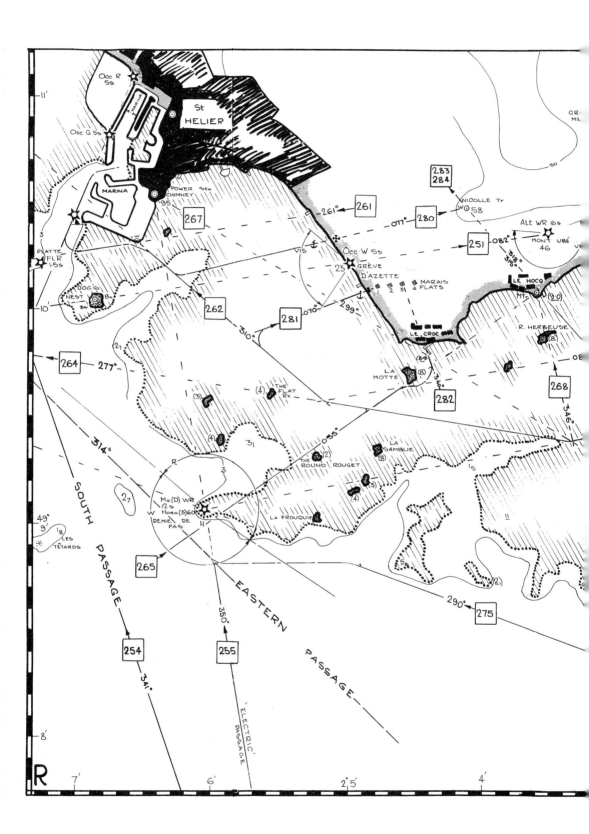

Occ R
5s

St
HELIER

Occ G 5s

MARINA

POWER Stn
CHIMNEY
95

267

PLATTE
FLR
1·5s
3

DOG'S
NEST
Bn

10

27

VIS

Occ W 5s

GREVE
D'AZETTE

23

261

077°

283
284

280

NICOLLE Tr
WⓄ 58

ALT WR 6s

MONT UBÉ
46

251

082°

318°
346°

LE HOCQ

MT
(9·0)

MARAIS
FLATS

LE CROC

R. HERBEUSE

262

281

070°

299°

310°

264

277°

LA
MOTTE

268

282

346°

THE
FLAT
Rk

08

314°

31

055°

LA
SAMBUE

THE
ROUND ROUGET

5

27

Mo (D) WR
12s
Horn (3) 60
DEMIE DE
PAS

W

R

3

LA FROUQUIE

11

265

290°

275

49°
9'
8
LES
TÉTARDS

SOUTH PASSAGE

EASTERN

350°

341°

PASSAGE

254

255

'ELECTRIC'
PASSAGE

8'

R

7'

6'

2·5'

4'

48A

CHART R Jersey, Demie de Pas and Violet Bank

Greve de Lecq, Jersey

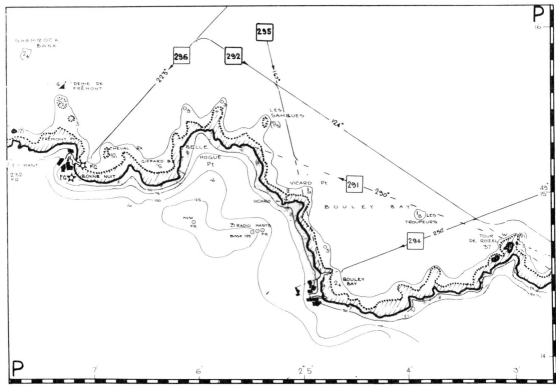

Chart P – Jersey, Bouley Bay

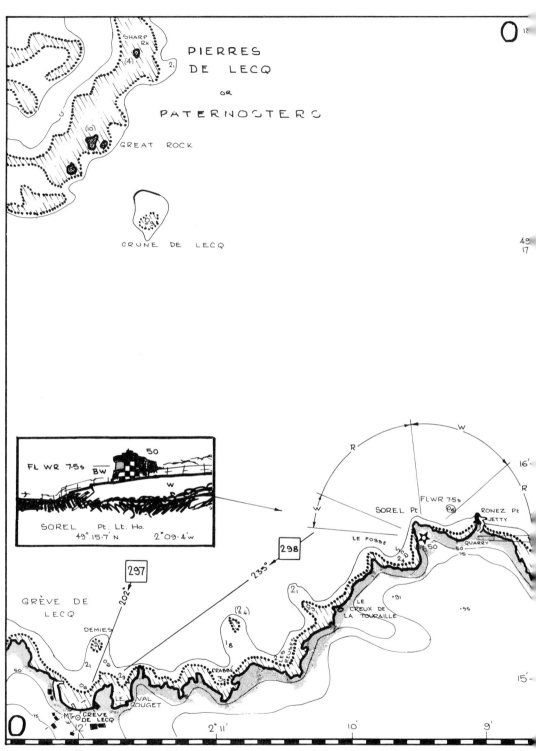

PIERRES
DE LECQ

OR

PATERNOSTERS

SHARP Rk

(4)

GREAT ROCK

(10)

65

CRUNE DE LECQ

FL WR 7.5s BW
50

W

SOREL Pt. Lt. Ho.
49°.15.7'N   2°09.4'w

W

R

W

16'

R

SOREL Pt

FL WR 7.5s

RONEZ Pt
JETTY

LE FOSSE

LECQ

50

QUARRY

50

75

298

235°

297

202°

GRÈVE DE
LECQ

DEMIES

(24)

2₁

5₅

LE
CREUX DE
LA TOURAILLE

·91

·55

·8

55

50

2₁

0·6

2·3

LES BRUSES

CRABBÉ

3₂

0·6

LE VAL
ROUGET

MTr O GRÈVE
DE LECQ
W 1·2

75

15'

2° 11'   10'   9'

O   18

49
17

Chart O – Jersey, Grève de Lecq

50A

Jersey's north coast

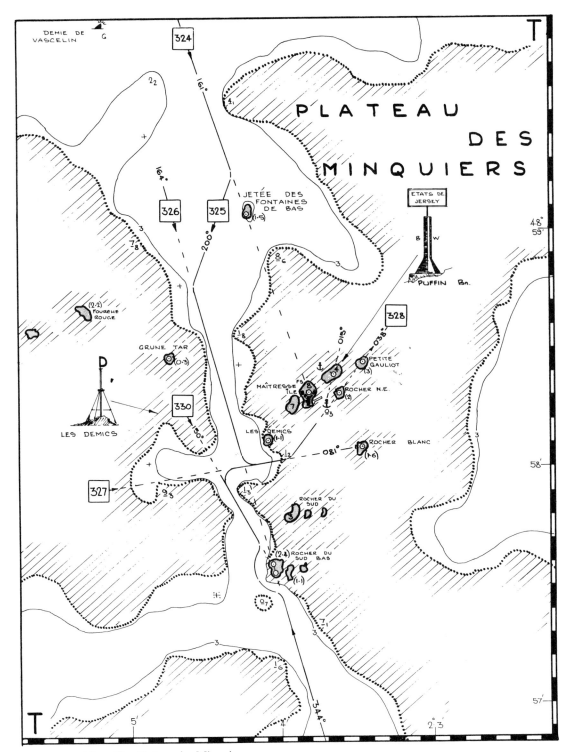

Chart T – Plateau des Minquiers

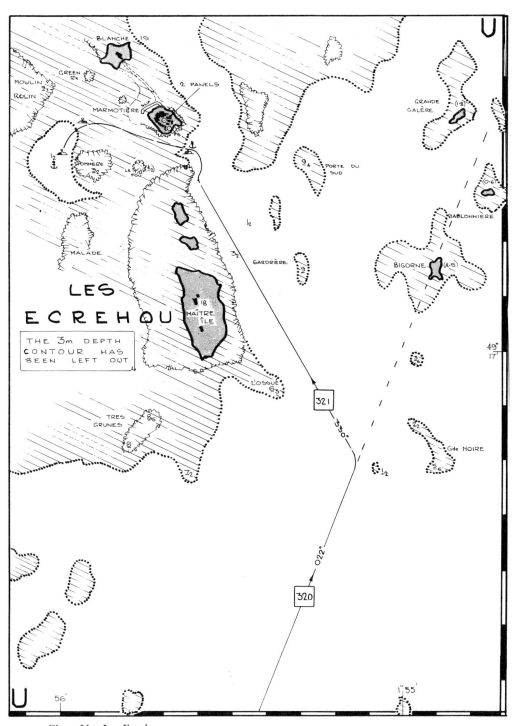

BLANCHE IS

GREEN Rk

MOULIN ROLIN

2 PANELS

MARMOTIÈRE

GRANDE GALÈRE (1·8)

POMMIÈRE

LE FOU

PORTE DU SUD

(0·6)

SABLONNIÈRE

MALADE

BIGORNE (4·5)

LES
ECREHOU

SARDRIÈRE

MAÎTRE ÎLE

THE 3m DEPTH CONTOUR HAS BEEN LEFT OUT

49° 17

L'OSSUE

321

330°

TRES GRUNES

Gde NOIRE

022°

320

1° 55′

Chart U – Les Ecrehou

1 Alderney

In an Alderney pub, a fisherman up from Jersey, after expressing his contempt of the tiny tides – half those at home – went across to Burhou for ormers. His *pannier à cou* full, he started back to Braye harbour on the low water. Two hours later having been swept nearly to Guernsey, the tide turned. Unable to make the Russel before his fuel ran out, his boat was carried up through the Race almost to Cherbourg. His mates ashore waved back as he passed rapidly down the Swinge again on the next ebb. Finally towed back to Braye, he staggered into the pub, far, far gone in thirst. Silently he bought a round of drinks.

Alderney has the most French looking town, St Anne, yet the most English population. The former, because it is a mere 9 miles across to France, yet 150 years of English garrison troops and a total evacuation during the last war have thinned out the Ridunians. But it is a charming island with friendly people and is the first of the Channel Islands to visit for most British yachtsmen. There are 14 forts, 13 pubs and the only railway in the Channel Islands.

Alderney folk are called Ridunians (Roman name *Riduna*) and now that we are here you might as well learn how to pronounce one or two of their rocks. From the harbour eastabout . . .

Saye bay	– Soy bay	Quoiré	– Quire	Coupé	– Coop
Grois rocks	– Groys	Noires Putes	– Nurpitz	Corbet	– Kerby
Brinchetais	– Brimtides				

Long may this individuality continue.

The approaches to Alderney are simple, for most of the island is steep-to and the only consideration is the fierceness of the tides. Though the range is half that of Jersey, the currents are up to 3 times that rate. You can imagine what it is like in the Swinge when a SW breeze meets a 7-knot ebb tide. Study the tidal charts inside the front and back covers and time your arrival or departure either at slack water or wind-with-tide. Like a rock in a river rapids, Alderney provides an eddy in the tide shadow at the NE and SW ends. On the up-tide ends the tide divides, flowing along each of the sides. The flood divides off les Étacs, locally called the Garden Rocks; the ebb divides at Sauquet, a *0.5m* rock off the lighthouse.

The main approach marks come first, by day then by night, and all aimed at Braye harbour; then we shall take a trip round the island. All Alderney marks are on Chart A p. 26A and all reference to tide times must necessarily be those of St Helier.

1 – From the North East or North

A single mark covers the whole of the N of the island,

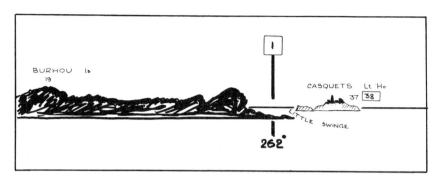

1 the Casquets × the N of Burhou. When the harbour opens up take

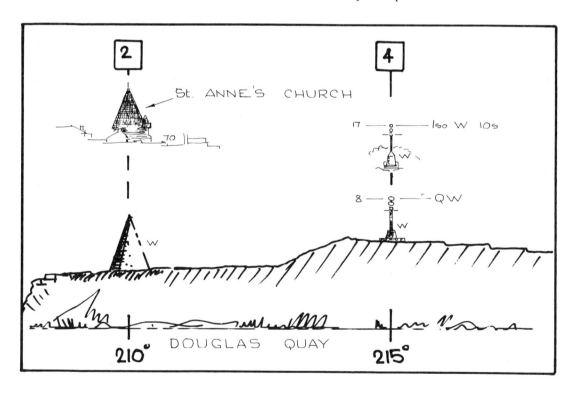

2 St Anne's Church × the white pyramid on Douglas quay. At night the same lines apply, but the sectored light on Château à l'Étoc keeps you clear of the end of the sunken breakwater. Enter on
4 (215°). Lights in line. If through bad timing, or you are sailing and perhaps the wind has

dropped, you find your boat being carried SW down the Race on the ebb, don't worry but later make the approach to the harbour from round the S instead. If this misfortune is at night, use the visible sector of Quenard LtHo to clear the dangers on the SE coast. In daytime your only anxiety is Bonit (*0·6m*). Here are the clearance marks

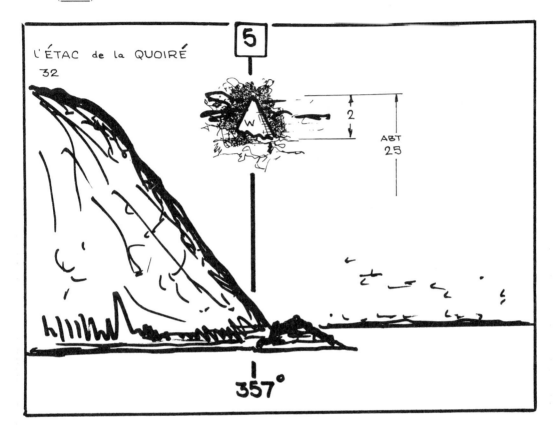

5 A white pyramid to the right of l'Étac de la Quoiré just clears to the E and

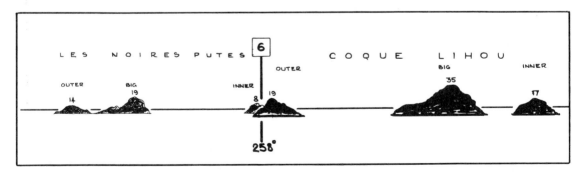

6 the inner Noire Pute × the outer Coque Lihou just clears to the S.

2 – From the South or South-West with entrance to BRAYE HARBOUR

This is the shortest and safest approach from Guernsey or la Déroute. The main mark is

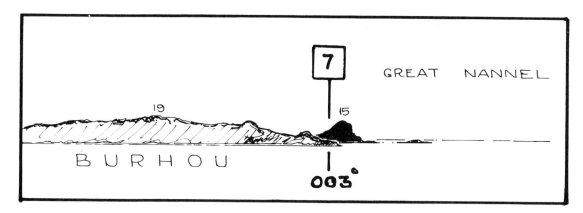

7 Great Nannel to the right of Burhou. A rather better mark at the top of the flood is

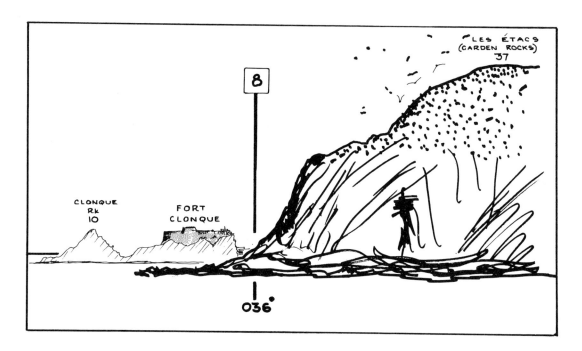

8 Fort Clonque to the left of les Étacs. These last rocks, locally called the Garden Rocks are the home of thousands of gannets. There is one very dangerous rock, Pierre au Vraic ($\underline{1 \cdot 2m}$) 2 miles WSW of les Étacs. It is not shown on Chart A and would only be a pest when sailing SW on the ebb. The key for its clearance is Fort Clonque.

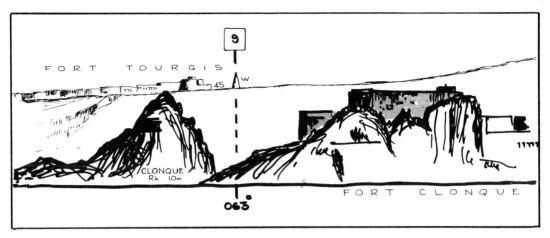

9 A white pyramid near Fort Tourgis to the left of Fort Clonque clears to the N: the S clearance is

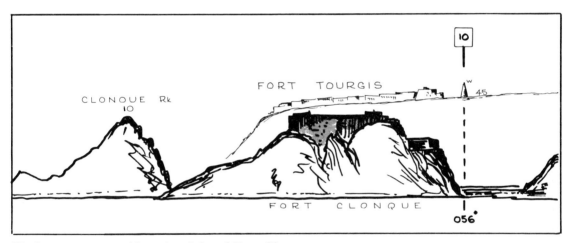

10 the same pyramid to the right of Fort Clonque.

Suppose you have timed your arrival in the Swinge too late on the ebb and haven't the wind or the power to carry on through. Then use this same transit 10 to lead into a snug anchorage ca. S or SW of Fort Clonque in Hannaine Bay. Even if it is blowing from the prevailing SW the outpourings of the Swinge during the low water act as a breakwater. The main tide in the Swinge will hit you hard on the ebb, but you can carry on up the W coast along line **7** (003°) Great Nannel to the right of Burhou, to another anchorage 1 ca. E of Barsier.

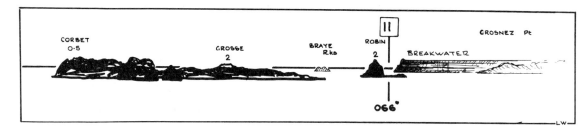

11 the end of the breakwater to the right of Robin. Both the Hannaine and the Barsier anchorages are normally to be used only to wait until half-tide up (St Helier), when you can carry on round to the harbour.

The S side of the Swinge is dominated by Corbet, 0·5m high, and its N clearance is

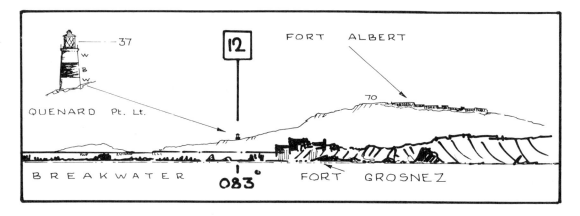

12 Quenard Lt, just seen to the left of Fort Albert as shown. If you have come in from the W, then

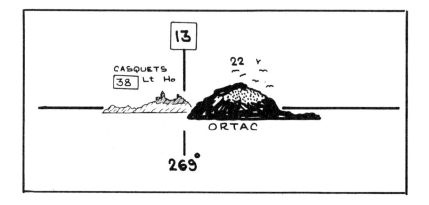

13 the Casquets LtHo S of Ortac is as good. Now come a couple of ca. to the N onto

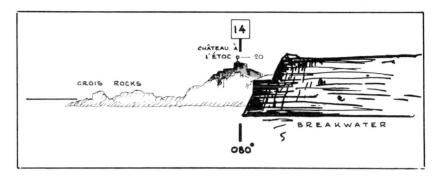

14 Château à l'Étoc × the end of the breakwater which clears N of Braye Rock. Pass N of the sunken remains of the breakwater on

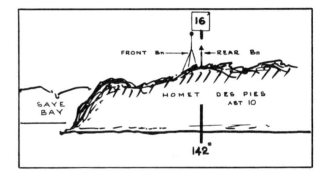

16 2 breakwater Bns in line. There is however a short-cut through the fallen debris

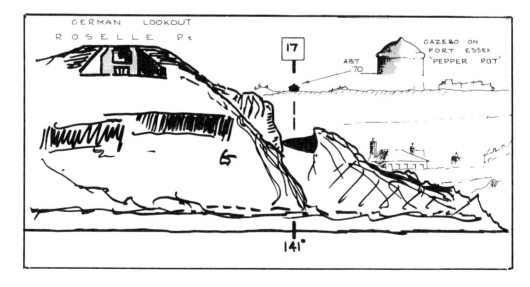

17 the 'pepper pot' on Essex Castle × a gap in the hillside below Fort Albert.

The only night transit in the Swinge is **12** (083°) Quenard Lt, just seen to the left of Fort Albert, p. 58. You then have to find your own way up the middle of the Swinge until you can turn E on the white sector of Château à l'Étoc and thus into the harbour.

Less exciting, however, is to stay in the Alderney Race, 7 miles wide, until you can work westward into the slack at the N of the island and use the approach from the N. The only danger on the Alderney side, Bonit, will be well below during the flood.

To complete the entrance to Braye harbour, little need be added. Anchor NW of a line of fairway buoys (see plan on Chart A, p. 26A), or if it blows hard from the NE, close under Fort Albert. In both positions there are mooring buoys for visitors. There is nowhere you may come alongside, for naturally commercial traffic must come first. All facilities can be found in Alderney, which has a friendly yacht club, good shops, an airport, hotels, restaurants, and hospitable people. There is a good chandler and with permission scrubbing may be carried out. Crabby harbour is reserved for local boats. Report to the Harbourmaster and Customs immediately.

The breakwater, a monument to My Lords of the Admiralty of 1847, is well worth a visit. Built against local advice without much thought of weather patterns, in 135ft of water, most of it was flattened 6 years after completion in 1864. Steamships and changing politics were the excuses for abandoning the outer half in 1900. Possibly the repair bill of £95,000 helped, too. After the last war, 4 million tons of stone were needed to heal a 50ft wound, but now a mere 30,000 tons a year keeps all concerned happy. There is a less expensive twin sister at St Catherine, Jersey, who at the turn of the century had consumed a mere £1000.

3 – Round the Island

There is much more to Alderney than remaining at anchor in Braye harbour and making a round of the pubs. So how about a trip round the island? We will go westabout from the harbour and the best time will be about half-tide down (St Helier) which gives us 9 hours before having to be back, just before high water. Naturally this needs an engine and settled weather, though there's nothing against anchoring in one of the bays for a night or two. Come out of the harbour as far as Corbet on the previous 3 marks:

17 (141°) the 'pepper pot' on Essex Castle × a gap in the hillside below Fort Albert, p. 59.

14 (080°) Château à l'Etoc × the end of the breakwater, p. 59.

12 (083°) Quenard Lt just seen to the left of Fort Albert, p. 58. Turn S on

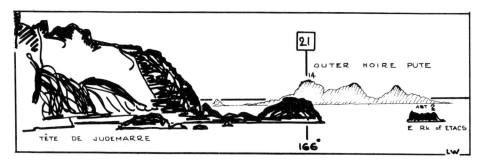

21 the outer Noire Pute × the SW cliff of Alderney. Stb'd a bit on

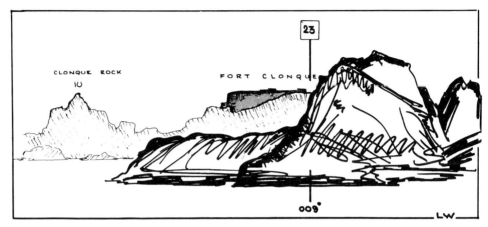

23 Fort Clonque × the large rock below Trois Vaux. Look now for gannets astern.

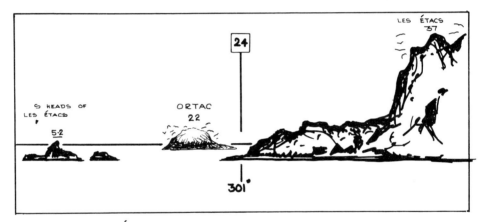

24 Ortac, seen to the left of les Étacs, which leads across a delightful low-water anchorage, Telegraph Bay. Now for a bit of rock-dodging on

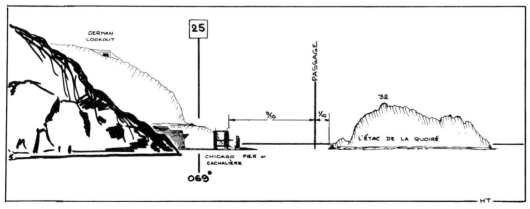

25 Cachalière pier just to the right of the shore. The granite quarry and ruined loading pier is

61

locally called 'Chicago' after the home town of its developer. Leave Fourquie 50m to port, but no more. From here on for 2 miles you have steep cliffs: keep between 100 and 150m off. To pass outside l'Étac de la Quoiré, 2ca. must be given to clear various boues. There is a passage between this mountain and the shore shown on line 25 – when the lower of 2 rungs of the staging is awash there is 2m.

A picnic anchorage is just below the white pyramid in line 5, p. 55, off the Blue Stone Beach, accessible only by boat.

Abreast of Longy Bay we come again on to coastal marks.

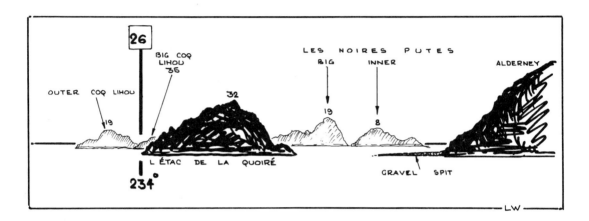

26 The outer Coque Lihou to the left of l'Étac de la Quoiré. Although strictly this would clear S of Boufresses, it is better to come out on

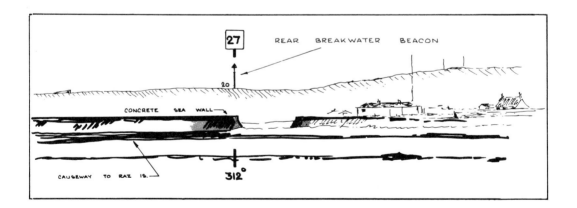

27 the rear breakwater Bn × a gap in the sea-wall in Longy Bay. Resume on

62

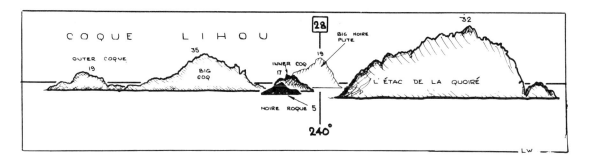

28 the big Noire Pute × the left of l'Étac de la Quoiré, which takes us comfortably outside the Brinchetais Ledge.

But before doing so, let's explore 2 anchorages. The first is Longy Bay,

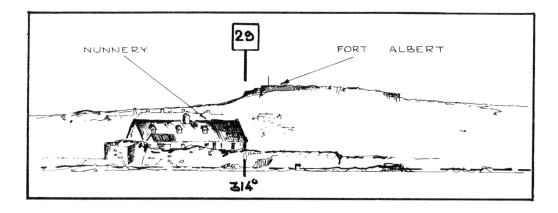

29 the left wall of Fort Albert × the Nunnery (Château de Longy). The second, in the lee of the Brinchetais Ledge, is Grounard anchorage,

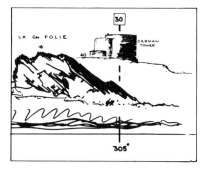

30 the German tower to the right of la Grande Folie. This conspicuous relic of the occupation dominates the NE of Alderney. Having rounded the Brinchetais Ledge, the NE clearance is

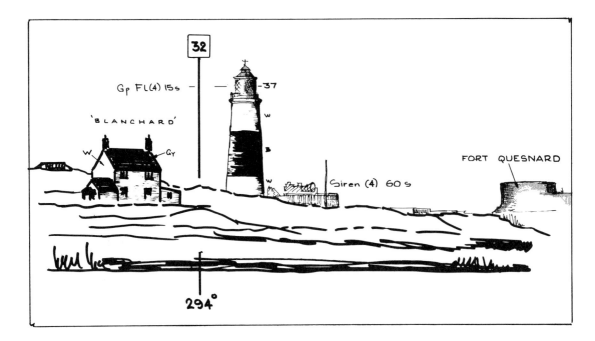

32 Quenard LtHo × a house ('Blanchard'). The next danger is Sauquet, the N clearance of which is

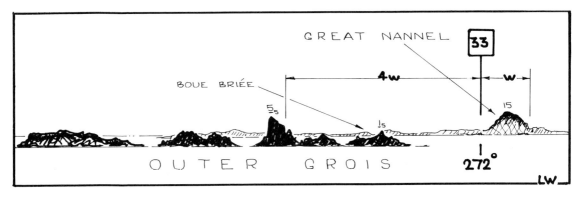

33 Great Nannel to the right of the Outer Grois. The E clearance is

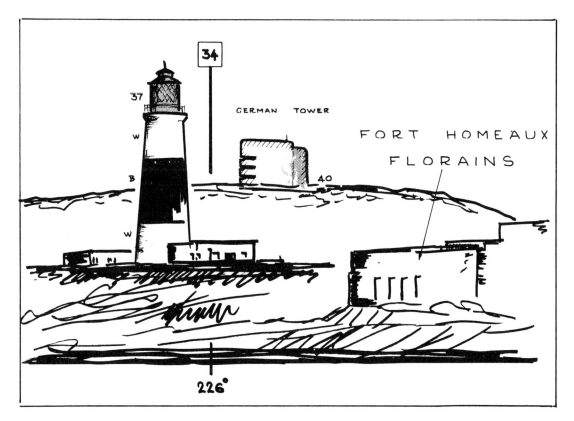

34 the German tower × Quenard LtHo. To pass inside Sauquet, take

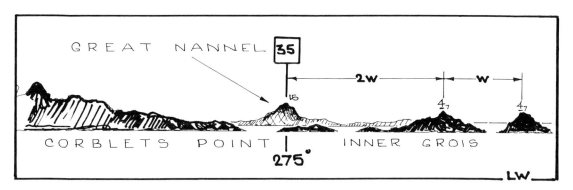

35 Great Nannel to the left of Inner Grois, a twin-headed rock, which also takes you S of Platte. There are 3 small bays here: Cat's Bay, Veaux Trembliers and Corblets, all sandy. Leave Corblets Bay on

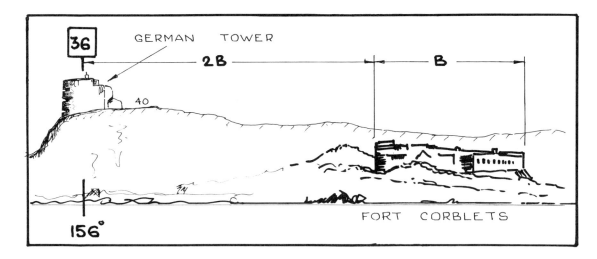

36 the German tower well to the left of Fort Corblets. The final mark to lead you back into the harbour is

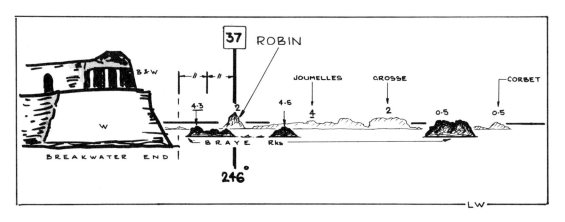

37 Robin, open to the right of the breakwater end. This mark is incidentally the reciprocal of line 11, p. 58. You can now re-enter Braye harbour using line 2, but if you do you will miss out Saye Bay, yet another sandy and sheltered cove entered between the high heads on both sides.

4 - Casquets

From Braye harbour to the Casquets is just over 7 miles and to pass a few hours there, through the low water, is an interesting trip for the adventurous. Admiralty chart 60 must be used for the approaches. Leave Alderney just after half-tide down so as to get there about low water, when the Petit Havre landing and anchorage is in the tidal lee of the rock.

Sail SW down the Swinge as before. Ortac 22m high, is steep-to on its S side, so leave it also 1 ca. to stb'd. Château à l'Étoc × the S side of Ortac clears 1 ca. S of l'Équêt *2·1m* a mile E of the Casquets. Both this rock and Fourquie *4·0m* should be showing by now; leave both 1 ca. to stb'd

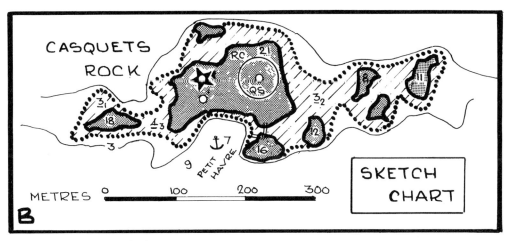

Chart B – Casquets sketch chart

and when the lighthouse bears about NNE head into the tiny harbour. I haven't drawn any marks for all this as it is all such open sea pilotage. But view 38 shows the lighthouse and very romantic it looks too. The sketch chart is a rough piece of information – after all, it isn't a place suitable for sculling around in a dinghy with a measuring tape.

This powerful first order light shares with Île d'Ouessant and Cap de la Hague guardianship of the Western Approaches. It was the first lighthouse in the Channel Isles, in 1726, and used 3 coal fires which were replaced by a multi-candle lamp in 1790; oil was used from 1799 until 1952, when the Casquets were electrified.

The curious use of 3 separate towers persisted right up to 1878. Their function was to give this important light some easily-detected 'characteristic' which was the only way before clockwork machinery and rotating lenses. Today 260 years later, in the 'dungeon' electronic equipment silently dispatches its radiobeacon Morse – QS.

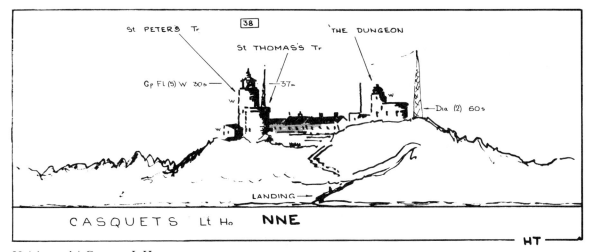

38 (view only) Casquets LtHo

2 Sark

Of all the islands, this is the least developed – not the same thing as being the most backward – and therefore most likely to stand up to the claims of the tourist brochures. The peaceful life, the horse traffic, the friendly people, the spring flowers, and the tiny bays – there they all are. Sark makes no provision for visiting yachts; we have no marina; the tiny Creux harbour can only hold very few boats and it dries. So it seems that the slow tempo of yachting will remain for some time. What a wonderful thought! *Chatchun bat sa maraïe* ('each of us chooses his own tide') say the Serquais.

Sark is the highest of the Channel Islands and unlike the others has steep cliffs all round the coast. Colonized from Jersey in 1566, the first job facing the citizens was to carve out an access tunnel inland from what today is Creux beach. In the cliffs are several sandy, snug coves, many excellent for overnight anchoring.

There is nothing difficult in arriving in daylight within a mile or two of Sark – the plateau is mostly between 75 and 100m high – but the cliffs are so featureless to a stranger that the final approach can be nerve-racking.

The position in the main tidal stream and the shape of the land cause strong currents; for example in the Gouliot, between Sark and Brecqhou it may touch 7 knots on the top of a big spring tide. Outside the harbours, the Goulet on the ebb reaches 6 knots.

The tidal currents close inshore vary too much to be shown on the tidal charts. But when coming from Guernsey, the decision whether to go N or S depends on the tide. Roughly it is slack water all round Sark at half tide. The fastest currents run about NE on the high water and SW on the low. Thus it follows that from the Bec du Nez to the Grand Moie it is slack at high water and from Sercul to Grande Grève it is slack at low water. Go N, therefore, coming from the Big Russel on the high water. But south-about on the low water. In fact, an hour after low water, from Sercul to the Creux harbour, there is a fair tide for 9 hours. When leaving from the harbours, St Peter Port bound, at between half-tide up and just before high water, go south-about. When clear of Sercul bear away for the Lower Heads buoy. Most other times, go N but if on the high water or soon after, circle the Bec du Nez and keep close to the Banquette Bay shore, keep lca. off the N of Brecqhou, leave Moie Batard ½ca. to port, then head W across the Big Russel. Naturally, wind direction must be considered in any inshore pilotage around Sark, and fortunately the high cliffs form a welcome lee. Both harbours are on the E, adjacent to each other, and the approaches are aimed there. Chart C, p. 28A.

1 – From the North

Day: The Bec du Nez is steep to on the N, so from Guernsey or the Big Russel the first 2 marks are

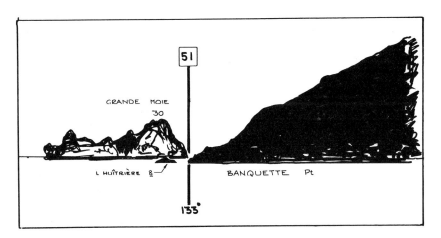

51 the right side of Grande Moie × Banquette Point, and

52 the left hump of Petite Moie × Noire Pierre. When l ca. off Noire Pierre, steer for the gap between the LtHo and Grande Moie: the dangers under the LtHo are cleared by

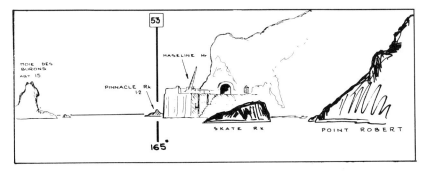

53 the Pinnacle Rock of the Goulet × the end of the Maseline jetty. Anchor anywhere NW of

Maseline jetty where shown. Coming alongside temporarily is possible, least depth 4m, but it is strictly reserved for commercial vessels. Don't anchor within 50m of the jetty or you will be in their way.

There is a local ordinance forbidding all traffic in the Goulet, so in order to reach the Creux harbour you must pass E of les Burons. Leave the Grande Moie 1 ca. to the N and pick up the following 3 marks:

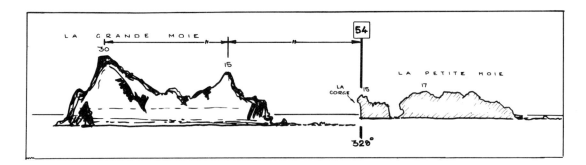

54 la Gorge open to the right of Grande Moie,

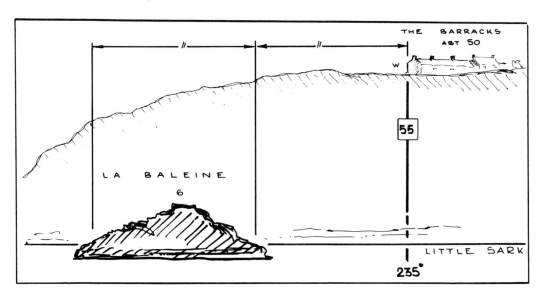

55 a long white house, 'The Barracks', to the right of Baleine,

56 the beach at the back of the harbour filling the entrance leads into Creux harbour.

Sark Ordinances control boats in Creux harbour and in the anchorage outside, les Lâches. You may dry out inside, or stay alongside, but the stone steps must at all times remain clear. At half tide there is about 4m between the pierheads; 2·7m at the stone steps; 1m at the iron ladder. Anchoring in les Lâches is forbidden W of the white patch on the pier heads. Prominent notices tell about all this. Water is from a tap and fuel is available from the Power Station. Between the Creux and Maseline harbours there is a building with lavatories, washing facilities and hot showers. It is half a mile up the hill to the shops and the pubs.

There are occasionally overfalls around the Bec du Nez, and a more open approach, particularly when sailing is

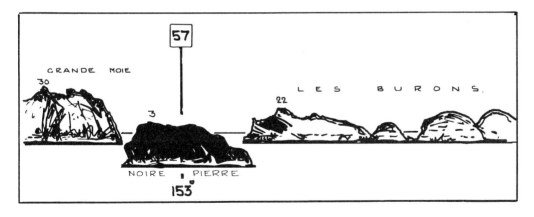

57 Noire Pierre, midway between the Grande Moie and les Burons. Pas ½ca. W of Noire Pierre and proceed as before.

Night: Making the harbours after dark is just possible, but on a dead black night should not be attempted until you have done it several times by day. The only practical way is northabout. If coming from St Peter Port, Chart Y, p. 32A, make a course roughly SE on **148** (306°) White Rock and Castle breakwater lights in line, p. 100. This transit takes you to the Lower Heads bell buoy and after rounding to the S of it, bring St Martin's Point LtHo to the same buoy, bearing 255°. This transit takes you into the white sector of Bec du Nez light, but you will have to carry on eastward and thence to the harbours without lights.

An alternative is to allow Grande Fauconnière, S of Herm, just to obliterate the Castle breakwater light, 271°. This clears N of the Bec du Nez, but you will have the passage from the Bec to the harbour to make in darkness. Near the Sark coast, it is not safe to use the obscured portion of Point Robert light (138°).

2 – From the North-east

Here is a nice long-distance and easily seen mark when coming from the Alderney Race:

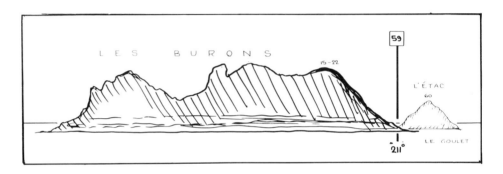

59 l'Étac to the right of les Burons. When 3ca. off les Burons, head for either harbour, but don't tangle with Founiais (*6·7m*).

3 – From the South-east

A single mark takes you almost into the Creux harbour,

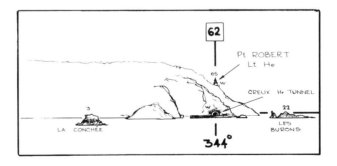

62 Point Robert LtHo × the Creux harbour tunnel. When Conchée bears SW the LtHo is lost behind the cliff, but from here to the harbour there are no dangers and you can use **56** (320°), the beach at the back of the harbour filling the entrance, p. 71.

4 – From the South

The most southerly rock off Sark is Sercul (*8·9m*), so with an offing of 2ca. look for

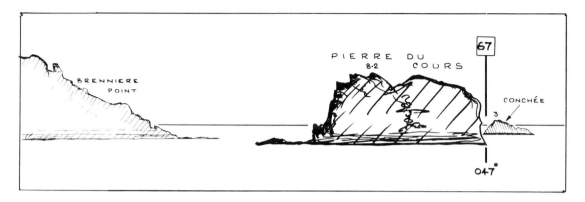

67 Conchée to the right of Pierre du Cours. Leave the latter, which is steep to nearly all round, 25m to port, and Brennière Point lca. and cross Baleine Bay. You may pass either side of Balmée, the inside channel being

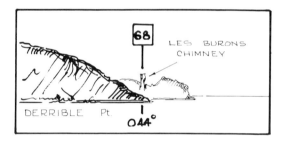

68 the 'chimney' of les Burons × Derrible Point. The hint that you have passed is

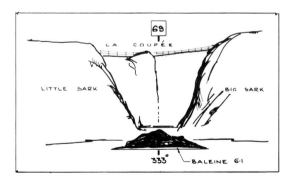

69 la Coupée × Baleine.

Pass about halfway between Conchée and Derrible Point to join **56** (320°) the beach at the back of the harbour filling the entrance, p. 71.

5 - ROUND the Island

You will have noticed that because Sark is tiny, the marks are shorter and possibly this is the charm from a yachtsman's view. Now we are going to take a trip around the island and seldom shall we be more than lca. from the shore. We shall start and finish at the Creux harbour. Remember that Little Sark is no place to be near the high water, and the N of the island is to be avoided on the low water. We shall suppose it is half-tide down, so we sail southabout.

Leaving les Lâches, steer for midway between Conchée and Derible Point. Derrible Bay, surrounded by cliffs, has no dangers except some small boues 10m SW of Derrible Point and is well suited for a night's anchorage. (The Cartographer, timid fellow, wrongly calls it Terrible.)

The next bay to the W, Dixcart, is also sandy, sheltered and 2 hotels nestle in the valley 10 minutes walk away.

All this part between the harbour and Brennière is sandy and overnight anchorage can be made in Pot Bay or, better, in Rouge Terrier. Any further S than this and the high-water swell will be unpleasant; there is a cliff path that leads up to a hotel, but no shops in Little Sark.

There is a boue lca. SW of Baleine cleared by

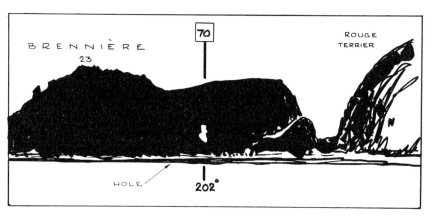

70 daylight just showing through a hole in Brennière. Make a handrail SE of Brennière on

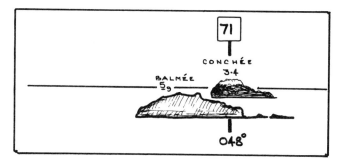

71 Conchée × Balmée. Pass inside Pierre du Cours and take a stern mark

74

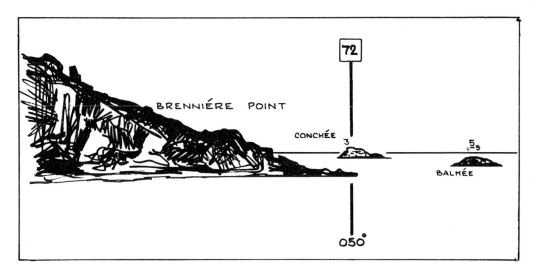

72 Conchée × Brennière Point. There are no marks from here to Port Gorey, but plenty of water, so steer carefully 300° midway between Moie de Viede 13m high and Pierre du Beurre _5·7m._ This channel is about 15m wide, so make sure the Guernsey packetboat isn't using it at the same time. Circle N and E of Moie de Port Gorey and clear off out to the NW on

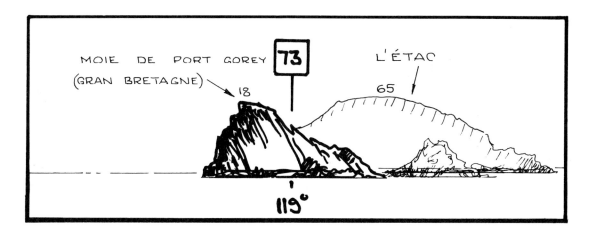

73 the left slope of l'Étac × Moie de Port Gorey (Grande Bretagne). The Tête d'Amont must on no account show to the left of Grande Bretagne. Carry on northwards, outside the Hautes Boues, using

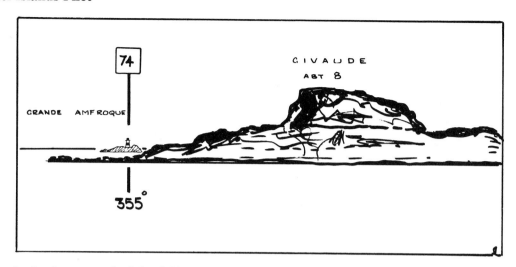

74 Grande Amfroque to the left of Givaude. But we shall continue close inshore. Maybe even drop anchor in Port Gorey, if it is neaps and settled. On the shore are the silver mines and in Port Gorey the remains of the loading quay. When you drop anchor there, think back 100 years and imagine coasters sailing out, loaded with ore.

Now comes a bit which requires, say, 4ft maximum draught and no higher than half tide – le Coursier. Creep out of Port Gorey: skirt the rocks on its northern arm and steer about N. All the time you must navigate by the colour of the water until the gateway of Moie de la Bretagne (port) and Adonis Pool (stb'd) is seen,

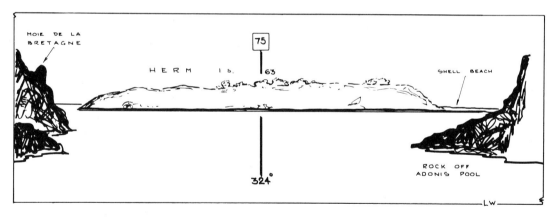

75 the high part of Herm, without the shell beach, fitting into the gateway. The channel dries _0·7m._ If you need a breather after this bit, Fontaine Bay is the place to anchor. If you don't like this last bit, simply circle outside Moie de la Bretagne and pass between Moie de la Fontaine and Baveuse. We are now in Grande Grève, the biggest and sandiest bay in Sark, where there is ample anchorage. Use for the southern entrance,

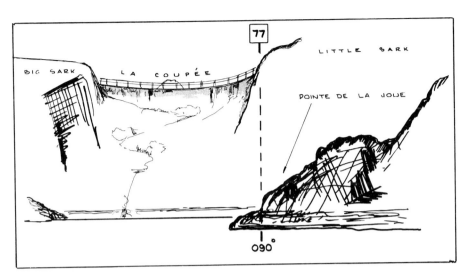

77 la Coupée × Pointe de la Joue, which passes S of Boue de la Baie. To clear the W of this boue and into Havre Gosselin take

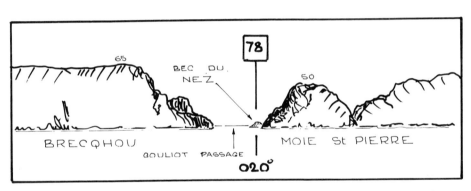

78 the Bec du Nez seen through the Gouliot Passage. Havre Gosselin is a snug anchorage, exposed only to the SW. It is Sark's only landing during those winter easterly gales when the Creux harbour is dry and la Maseline is a boiling whirlpool. There are steps and an iron ladder, both good for dinghy landing. If you feel up to the 299 steps there is a most friendly pub at the top which provides meals.

The passage through the Gouliot merely requires a tide table; the least depth is 4·3m. It is clean on both sides, but watch out for a boue *1·2m* just SW of Moie St Pierre. Half tide is slack water, and the strongest current is at the top of big springs, 7 knots, northerly.

Once through the Gouliot, westbound, don't turn off for Herm too smartly – the Boue de Gouliot 0·9m waits. When St Martin's Point, Guernsey, is seen N of Moie Batard, NW of Brecqhou, you are clear. Landing on Brecqhou is not possible: the island is private.

Four small bays follow now in quick succession: Port à la Jument, Pegane Bay, Port de Moulin and Saignie. All are shingle but fair holding and quite suitable for a night anchorage in offshore settled weather.

A single mark clears to the W of all the dangers in Banquette Bay and the Bec du Nez

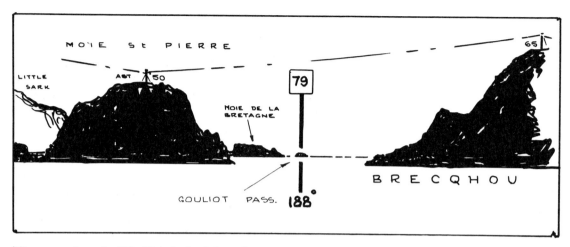

79 any rock to the W of Little Sark just showing through the Gouliot Passage. From the Bec SE back to the harbour, the same marks may be used as in the approach on p. 69. However, at neaps les Fontaines Bay is useful even at low water – the Demie $5 \cdot 4m$ is a middle-of-the-bay danger. The best anchorage, and one away from traffic and swell, is Grève de la Ville, where close in to some stone steps it is shingle and sand in 7m. A cliff path leads quite close to a pub which serves meals, and shops are nearby. From here to the Creux has already been described, p. 70.

One final word about Sark. Because you don't see officials in peaked hats, because you don't fill in forms, because you are left to your own devices, this doesn't mean you can do what you like. Dogs have been shot for illegal landing, yachtsmen have been shoved in the jail, boats obstructing the quays have been cast adrift. Sark is self-governing and acts swiftly against anyone becoming a pest.

3 Herm

How fortunate is Guernsey in having Herm right on her doorstep – just far enough to be interesting, yet just big enough to support a tiny population. Bought by the States from the Crown after the war, Herm is a part of Guernsey though controlled by a tenant who, wisely, has restricted development. A delightful piazza surrounded by intriguing little shops is only a few yards from an hotel, the restaurant and the pub. Services are still held in the miniscule 12th-century Chapel next to the Manor in the centre of the island. Jethou, and its two satellites Crevichon and Grand Fauconnière, are private and landing is forbidden.

Everything about Herm is in miniature, so the transits are short and numerous. We can regard Herm as the centre of a long reef stretching from the NE (Grande Amfroque) through the Humps, Herm, Jethou, the Ferriers, les Barbées, Musé: the Lower Heads bell buoy marks the SW end. On the E of the island there are no Bns as the Big Russel is wide and seldom used by commercial traffic. On the W, in the Little Russel, most of the Bns are shown on view 131, p. 94. The best way to learn your way around Herm is to treat it as a series of channels through from the Little to the Big Russel. Charts D and E, p. 30A.

Alligande passage may be used at night, but only in summer; all the rest are strictly daylight only. Many marks around Herm use the churches in St Peter Port, so all these are shown on a single profile view on Chart G p. 34A. Though the 9 routes are given from the Little to the Big Russel they can just as readily be used in the reverse direction. All are frequently used under sail. The least depths are given after each title.

Along the Big Russel shore of Herm and the Humps, the tidal current runs nearly the same as in the Big Russel itself (see tidal charts inside the front and back covers). But in the Percée passage it runs SE for 9 hours starting about LW; and 3 hours NE from half-tide down. In the Neck of Jethou, which is awash at half-tide, the tide runs always in one direction – E.

1 – MUSÉ PASSAGE (12m)

Between the Lower Heads bell buoy and the entire group of rocks S of Jethou there is a half-mile wide passage. The N side is marked by a post with a letter M, which stands for Musé, though the Bn is actually on the Demi Ferrière rock.

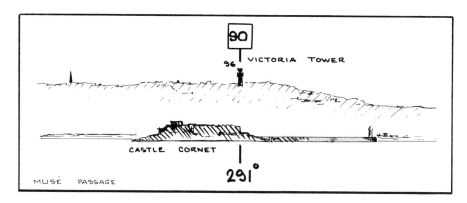

90 Victoria tower × N face of Castle Cornet.

2 – PARFONDE PASSAGE (2·8m)

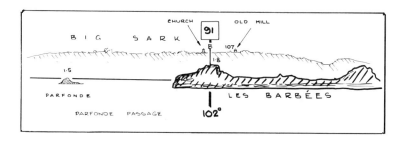

91 Sark church × less Barbées Bn. A cable before the Bn, Chart E, p. 30A, borrow to the N so as to leave the N face of the rock on which the beacon stands 10–20m away. Once past the rock by ½ca. take

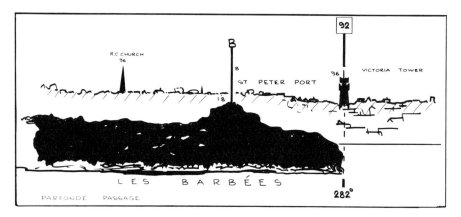

92 Victoria tower × N face of les Barbées. This mark must be held for another 7ca. to clear S of les Anons (*3·3m*).

Looking southeast from St Peter Port over the Russel Channel.

3 – TOBARS PASSAGE (5·0m)

This is commonly used by the Guernsey-Sark steamers. Chart E, p. 30A.

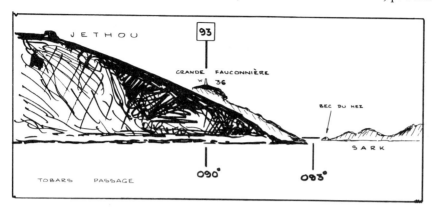

93 Bec du Nez, Sark × S of Grande Fauconnière. In poor visibility you can put Grande Fauconnière white Bn ('pepper pot') by the S slope of Jethou. When about 2ca. short of Jethou, turn to stb'd on

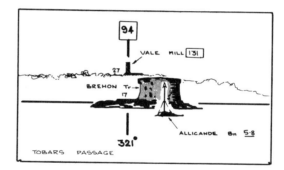

94 Vale Mill to the left of Brehon Tower. Two ca. later, turn sharply to port on

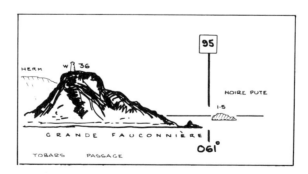

95 Noire Pute × SE of Grande Fauconnière. The S of Grande Fauconnière is steep-to, so ½ca. off is plenty. If you want to take a short cut N of les Barrarettes (Quarter Rocks), use a stern mark.

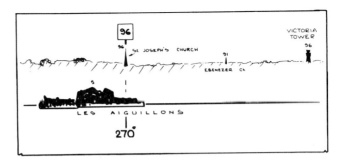

96 St Joseph's Church × N face of les Aiguillons. This mark does not however clear S of Grande Fauconnière.

4 – CORBETTE PASSAGE (2·2m)

Here is the obvious route from St Sampson to Sark and since it has no dog-leg it can easily be sailed. Look for the first mark when about 3 ca. NW of Corbette de la Mare Bn, and which should be located when no nearer than about 3 ca. NW of Corbette Bn, view 131, p. 94, Chart E, p. 30A.

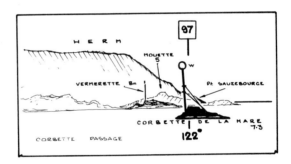

97 Sauzebourge Point, Herm × Corbette de la Mare rock. Leave the Corbette rock, which is steep-to on its SW side, 20–30m to port and come on to

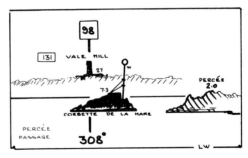

98 Vale Mill × Corbette de la Mare Bn. This transit takes you clear of everything right into the Big Russel though not as far as the Fourquies of Herm, p. 98. The mill and the Bn may, in fact, coincide all the way from Corbette to Epec, but they must be open left as drawn, by about the elevation of the mill, in order to pass Percée rock and the sandbank S of Mouette.

5 – PERCÉE PASSAGE (3·4m)

Since this is but an extension of the Corbette passage, all you have to do is to keep clear of the Big Russel dangers at the exit. The key to this is Hermetier (Rat Island) and the eastern clearance is

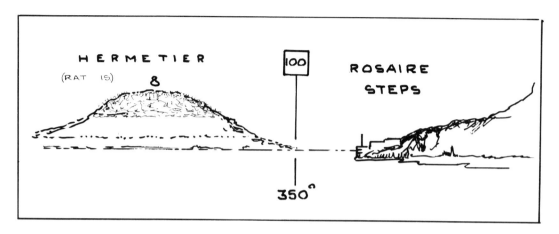

100 Hermetier open to the left of Rosaire steps. This clears to the W of Meulettes. Don't turn E until

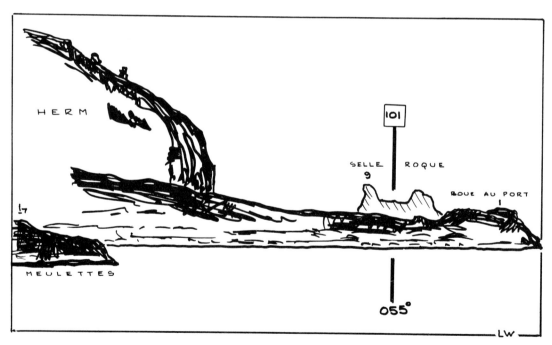

101 Selle Roque × Boue au Port. The W clearance is

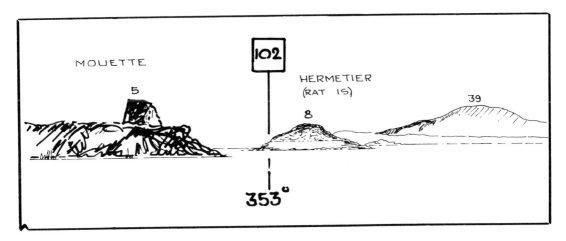

102 Rat Island to the right of Mouette. The main transit is (308°) Vale Mill × Corbette de la Mare Bn, line 98 p. 83 – i.e. the Corbette Passage, but renamed here as Percée.

6 – The NECK of JETHOU (5·0m)

This short cut can only be used towards the high water and the tide sets through it always eastwards. Look for the stern mark when about ½ca. S of Alligande Bn.

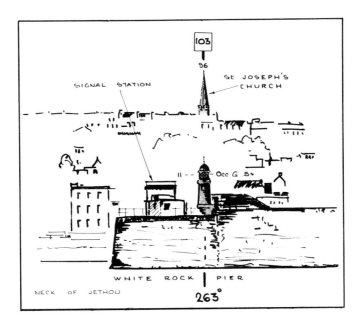

103 St Joseph's church × White Rock L. Leave the private landing pier on Jethou 30m to port and continue eastwards to join **98** (308°) Vale Mill × Corbette de la Mare Bn, p. 83.

7 – ALLIGANDE PASSAGE (0·5m)

This is the most direct route from Town to Herm harbour and the only one possible at night. It isn't too good near low water as you will see from Chart E, p. 30A,

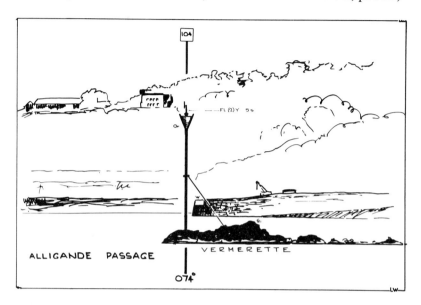

104 White patch on Herm quay – Vermerette Bn.

8 – CREUX PASSAGE (3·0m)

This is the low-water passage from Town to Herm. It starts off by a mark to clear Foutu, a drying rock S of Brehon Tower, Chart E, p. 30A.

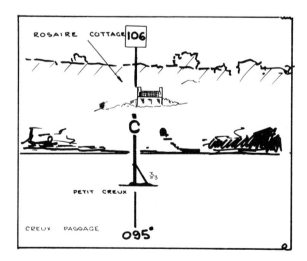

106 Rosaire Cottage (red roof) × Creux Bn. Make a handrail about 25m N of Petit Creux rock, on which the Creux Bn stands, and take a stern mark

86

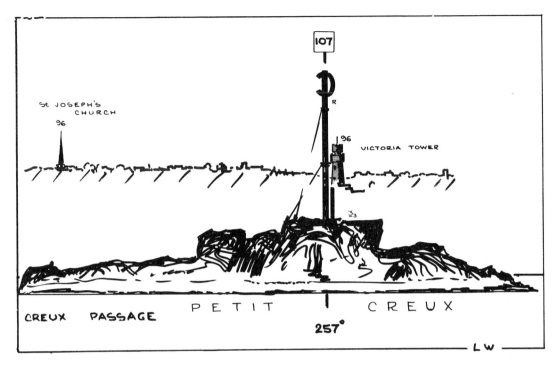

107 Victoria Tower × Creux Bn. After 2 ca., take a second stern mark

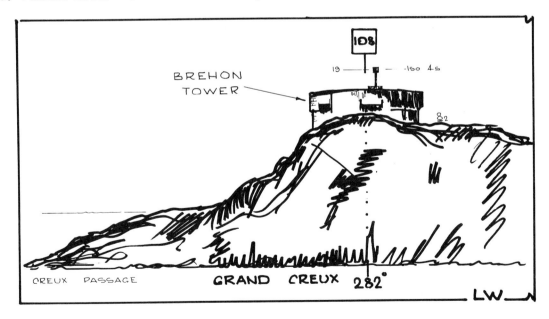

108 Brehon Tower × the high part of Grand Creux, which joins the Corbette passage.

9 – LE BOURSÉE (HAYES PASSAGE) (10m)

This passage is best used below half tide. Above this, not only are the key rocks covered, but the currents are fierce and come from umpteen different directions. Start off S of Tautenay, view 131, p. 94, Chart D, p. 30A.

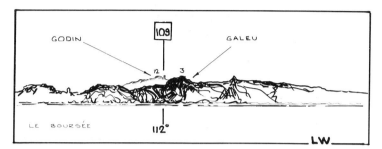

109 Godin just to the left of Galeu. Look for a stern mark when 3 ca. off Galeu Island,

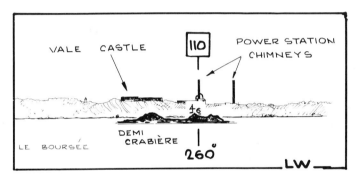

110 the left one of 2 chimneys × the north head of Demi Crabière. Again a stern mark

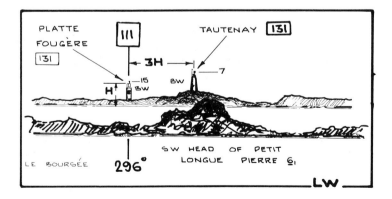

111 Platte Fougère open to the left of Tautenay. This mark clears you out into the Big Russel. If you are foolish enough to be battling around here on high water you can use, since the Demi Crabière will then be covered,

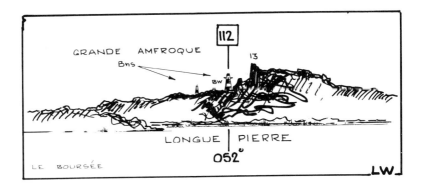

112 Grande Amfroque Bn to the left of Longue Pierre rock. This isn't a transit so much as a turning point, and you will have to leave Galeu peak (Pierre de la Moue) a fairly exact ½ ca. to port before taking up line **111** (296°) Platte Fougère open to the left of Tautenay, p. 88.

10 – HERM HARBOUR and ROSAIRE STEPS

Herm has a tiny, snug harbour built by quarrymen in the early 1800s. It is very crowded above half tide. The entrance is N of Vermerette, Chart E, p. 30A.

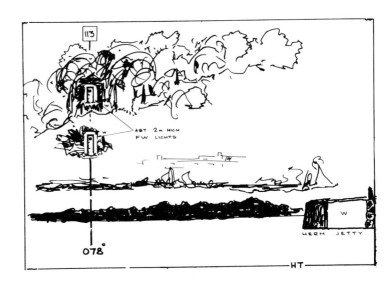

113 2 white Bns in line. These are lit throughout the summer at night. When Vermerette rock is awash, there is a metre at the end of Herm quay. Below half tide use the Rosaire steps 2½ca. S of the quay. Approach this landing from the S or from the Percée passage, p. 84. There is about a 20-minute overlap between the top landing at Rosaire being covered and Vermerette rock signalling the depth in Herm harbour. Good anchorage, though crowded, can be found in the bight W of Rosaire steps, but when the drying area between Vermerette and Herm is well covered the southerly stream may reach 3 knots. There are no facilities, except food and drink, unless you include a tiny jail.

11 – Round the Island

This section might well be called 'Rocks I have Hit' because, as is well known, that is the most expensive and therefore the finest way to learn. As you can see, Herm is deep to the S, while at the N some 3 square miles are more or less dry. The northern third of Herm itself is sand, as are all the beaches – Belvoir, Shell Beach and Mouisonnière, along the N, besides Vallois at the NW, named after the people of the adjacent Guernsey parish of Vale.

Coming out of Herm harbour, before we go round the island, there are 2 tiny anchorages to investigate before setting off southabout. The first is a high-water picnic spot N of Hermetier. I don't show a view but it uses 2 man-made objects, les Barbèes bn, (line 92, p. 80) × Vermerette (view 131, p. 94). The second, for use only at low water, is 1 ca. E of the Roquerie. Starting from just N of Vermerette

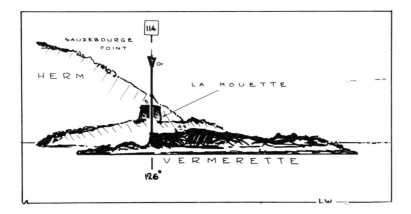

114 la Mouette × Vermerette. Then take

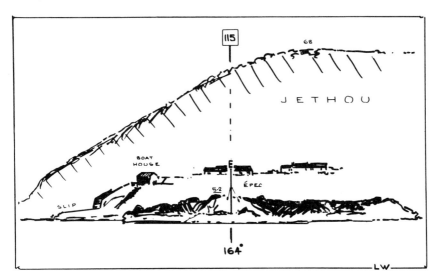

115 a house on Jethou × Épec Bn. Time and tide wait for no man, so off we go SE on **98** (308°)

Vale Mill × Corbette Bn, p. 83. Clear S of the Meulette on **101** (055°) Selle Roque × Boue au Port, p. 84. Selle Roque, which indeed looks like a saddle, may be passed either side. If going inside

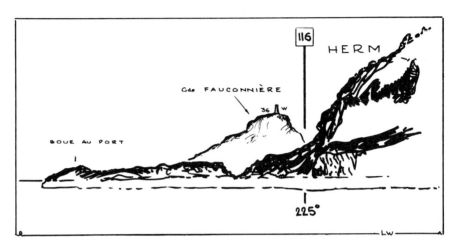

116 Grande Fauconnière × the SE cliff of Herm, which also clears outside Putrainez. Leave Caquorobert 1 ca. to port and you can anchor in Belvoir Bay (Chart D, p. 30A).

This area from here N for some 2 miles is like the Minquiers – high rocks and sandy beaches with the tide rushing down the channels. Needless to say, all this part is a playground for small boats, but only at low water: the bigger the tide the better. There are certain places where you can sit on a sand spit and look N level with the surface of the sea, while 10m away there is a waterfall. At low water the current runs from the N, southward through any channel it can find. From Belvoir Bay you can edge along the Shell Beach using eyeball navigation, to where there is a secure picnic anchorage below half tide just SE of Alderney Corner.

How about a trip up to the Humps? Start off from Belvoir Bay near low water

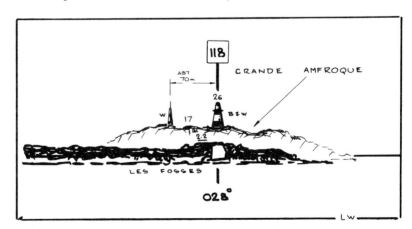

118 Grande Amfroque Bn × a metre square rock in les Fosses: for some reason this rock doesn't grow vraic like all the adjacent reef. To make the port turn into the Usurie passage,

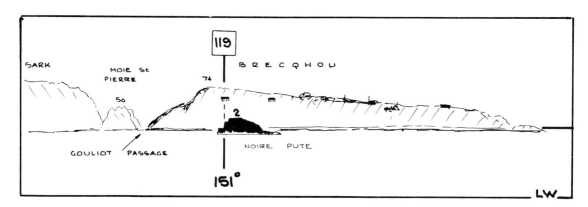

119 the more easterly of 2 cottages in Brecqhou × a particular part of the NE face of Noire Pute. Make the small westerly diversion as shown and end up in a beautiful anchorage called Godin. To return to Herm, continue southabout round Canouette, 12m high; then 3ca. NW – there is plenty of water now – then 205° and back to Alderney Corner. This 205° part is like a 75m-wide 'river', the banks of which are sand and rocks, down which flows the current at 5 knots.

You are now ready to venture up another 'river', just W of Banquette *3·1m* when low water is the only possible time – other times you can't tell where the channel sides are. From Alderney Corner you can see a tree 10m high and as wide, above Belvoir Bay. I am all against trees as marks, but put this

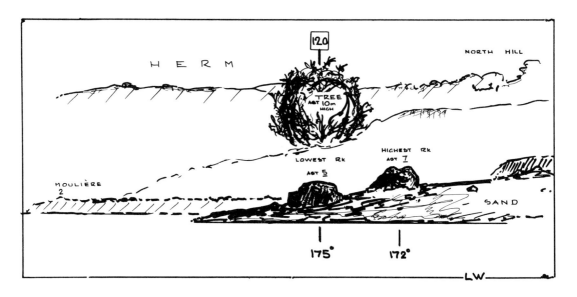

120 tree above Belvoir Bay × rocks on Alderney Corner. Proceed 'up-river' (against the tide) leaving Banquette a metre or so to stb'd and in the middle of the 'river bed' gradually bringing the tree × the highest of the 2 rocks. You will have ample steerage way against a 4-knot tide. When Tautenay, view 131, p. 94, is about 4ca. off, take a port turn on to

92

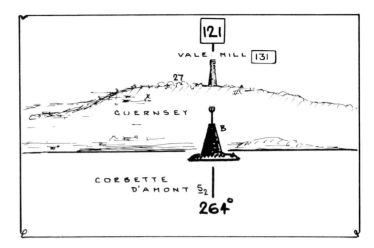

121 Vale Mill × Corbette d'Amont Bn, both on view 131, p. 94. This takes you back into the Little Russel where you can rejoin the NW end of the Corbette passage, p. 83, but just before this, when abreast of Roustel, there is a final mark, Chart F, p. 32A,

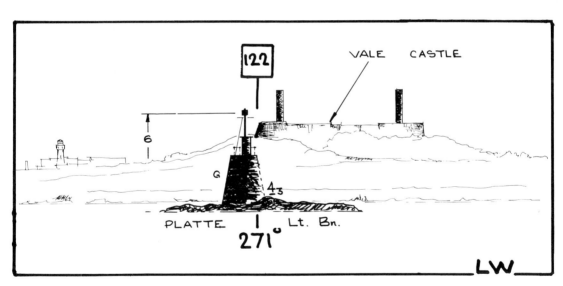

122 the S face of Vale Castle × Platte Lt Bn, which leads into a picnic anchorage among the sand bars of the N end of Herm, Chart E, p. 30A.

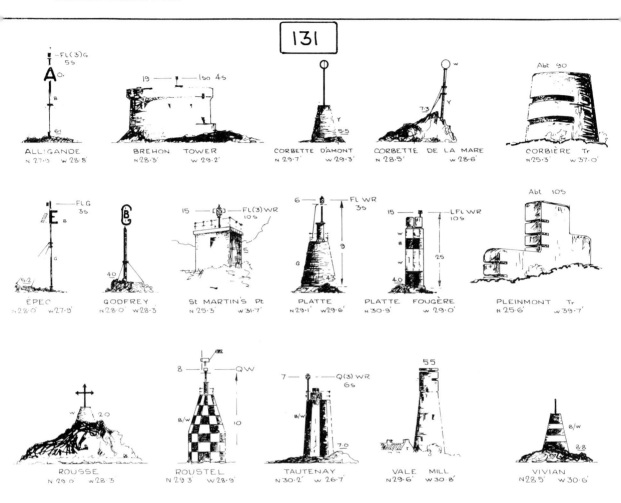

131

ALLIGANDE — FL(3)G 5s
N 27·0   w 28·8

BREHON TOWER — 19 — Iso 4s
N 28·3'   w 29·2'

CORBETTE D'AMONT
N 29·7'   w 29·3'

CORBETTE DE LA MARE
N 28·5'   w 28·6'

CORBIÈRE Tr — Abt 90
N 25·3'   w 37·0'

ÉPEC — FLG 3s
N 28·0'   w 27·9'

GODFREY
N 28·0'   w 28·3

St MARTIN'S Pt — 15 — FL(3)WR 10s
N 25·3'   w 31·7'

PLATTE — 6 — FL WR 3s
N 29·1'   w 29·6'

PLATTE FOUGÈRE — 15 — LFL WR 10s
N 30·9'   w 29·0'

PLEINMONT Tr — Abt 105
N 25·6'   w 39·7'

ROUSSE
N 29·0   w 28·3

ROUSTEL — 8 — QW
N 29·3'   w 28·9'

TAUTENAY — 7 — Q(3) WR 6s
N 30·2'   w 26·7'

VALE MILL — 55
N 29·6'   w 30·8'

VIVIAN
N 28·5'   w 30·6'

View 131

94

4 Guernsey

What Sark is to Alderney, so Guernsey is to Jersey – softer, less commercialized and quieter. By an historical fluke, shipbuilding and granite were important in the nineteenth century and have left 2 magnificent harbours. St Peter Port handles passengers and containers, leaving St Sampson for oil, coal, timber and stone. Perhaps this is why the Guernsey yachtsman is so well looked after – 4 marinas, for example. Visitors in boats are shrewdly welcomed; you spend money without straining the public services; you neither clog up other travellers nor occupy valuable hotel beds.

Guernsey is stuck out in the main tidal stream as much as Alderney, but since the shape is different, the coastal tides aren't as swift. The tidal charts show all but the close inshore currents, and seldom do these exceed 2 knots; the important tides being in the Little Russel. Roughly half tide is slack water between Herm and Guernsey or Sark and Herm. Within 3ca. of the steep S cliffs there is 5 hours of lee from the general SW direction of the low water. Along the NW side, close inshore, the current runs for 6 hours from high-water SW; then 6 hours NE starting at low water.

Most of the main day and night approach marks are on Chart Y, p. 32A. Herm and the channels through between the Big and Little Russels are treated separately pp. 96–97 and Chart F, p. 32A.

Sixteen prominent objects in Guernsey and Herm are on view 131, p. 94.

1 · LITTLE RUSSEL from North (2·1m)
(West of Roustel)

Day: It is fortunate that St Peter Port, unlike St Helier, both faces E and is also sheltered by a group of islands (Herm, etc.). The main mark

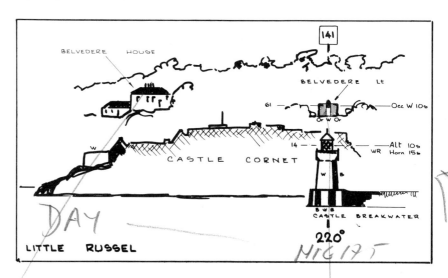

141 Belvedere Lt × Castle Breakwater Lt, passes only 5ca. NW of Platte Boue *(1·8m)*, but if you can see the mainland of Sark to the E of Grande Amfroque, you are clear. Two bns in line at 152° on Grande Amfroque, Chart D, p. 30A, strike this rock.

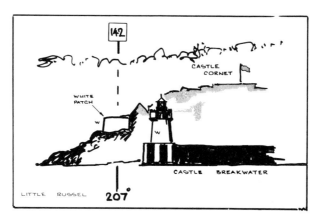

142 Castle Cornet white patch × Castle Breakwater Lt clears all the drying dangers in Belle Grève Bay, Chart G, p. 34A.

Night: The same transit is used, much easier to see by night than by day. A most useful nearer alternative is to put Brehon and Roustel Lts, view 131, p. 94, in line at 198°. Coming in from NW you are safe in the visible sector of Sark light (at least 138°). As the main transit passes plumb over Agenor (2·1m), you must borrow to the SE ½ca. when abreast of Brehon Tower. The red sector of Platte guards Agenor.

2 – LITTLE RUSSEL from North (6·0m)
(East of Roustel)

Day: This is more easily seen from a distance than the preceeding mark.

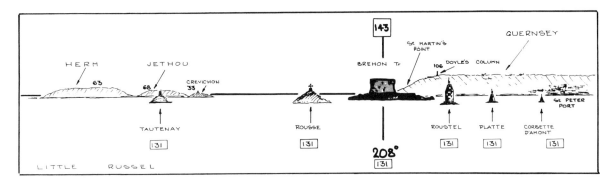

143 St Martin's Point just to the right of Brehon Tower, Chart F, p. 32A. Two ca. before coming to Roustel change to

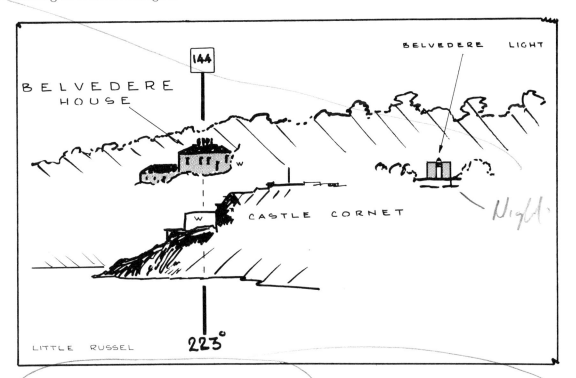

144 Belvedere House × Castle Cornet white patch. Chart G, p. 34A.
Night: Nothing doing – use line **141** (220°) Belvedere Lt × Castle Breakwater Lt, p. 96.

3 – LITTLE RUSSEL from South

Day: No marks are needed and you can enter anywhere between St Martin's Point and Lower Heads buoy. To clear E of all the dangers to within half a mile of St Peter Port,

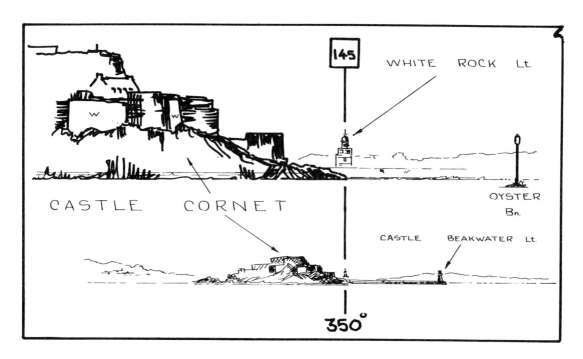

145 White Rock Lt to the right of Castle Cornet (Chart Y, p. 32A).

Night: Making a night landfall anywhere near St Martin's Point, make sure that you can see les Hanois Lt. The obscured sector covers most of the dangers S of Guernsey. The red sector of St Martin's Lt is only to guard the rocks just off the point, so come to the E until White Rock light is just visible to the E of Castle Point, which is the same as line 145.

4 – BIG RUSSEL from Northward
(with St Peter Port Entrance)

Day: If I were driving a fully rigged three-master with a St Trinian crew, then I might approach St Peter Port from the Big rather than the Little Russel. The channel between Herm and Sark is seldom narrower than $2\frac{1}{2}$ miles and is very nearly free of all dangers. If, however, you are tacking against a brisk south-westerly there is no better way to reach the comforting lee of St Martin's Point. The only dangerous rock in the Big Russel is les Fourquies (of Herm) (*2·3m*). It is clear lca. all round but so isolated that I give striking marks, Chart E, p. 30A: though there is a Card N buoy, these marks remain of great use in tacking either SW or NE past this isolated rock.

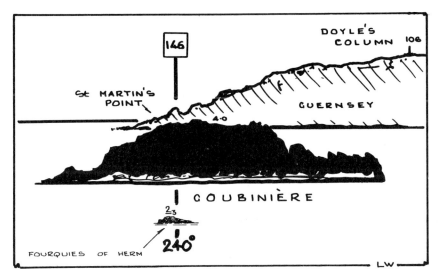

146 St Martin's Point × Goubinière and

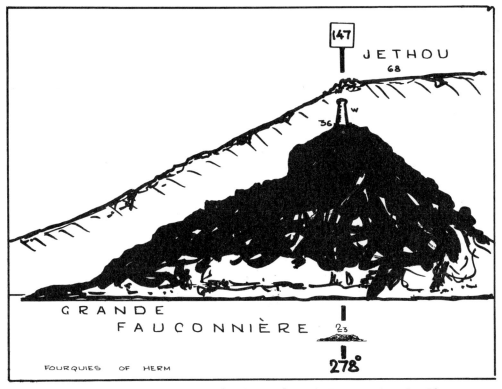

147 a cluster of rocks on the S slope of Jethou – Grande Fauconnière Bn. If you can see Brehon Tower between Herm and Jethou, you are comfortably clear to the NE. Once round the Lower Heads buoy you can head off to St Peter Port.

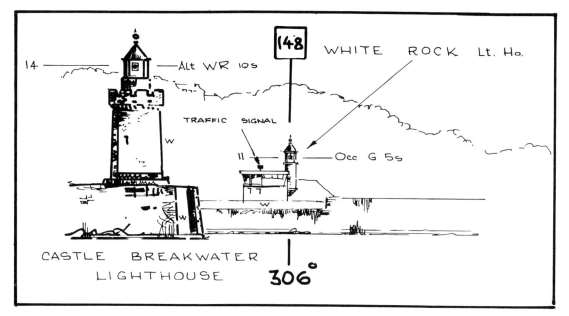

148 St Peter Port pierheads open clears the rocks off Castle Cornet (Chart G, p. 34A).
Night: At night use the white sector of Noir Pute light as far as the Lower Heads buoy, then turn NNW up the Little Russel to St Peter Port, Chart Y p. 32A. Leave the buoy as close as you like to stb'd and line up the White Rock and Castle Breakwater Lts, shown on view 148.

Traffic signals are in operation on the signal station on the White Rock.

Red light visible from seaward – no entry.

Red light visible from inside – no exit.

Boats less than 18m long and under power are accepted at their own responsibility, but this does not include yachts under sail. There is a speed limit of 4 knots. At the harbour mouth you may be hailed by the signal station and told where to berth.

St Peter Port has all the amenities of the capital for an island of 50,000 inhabitants. You can't go alongside in the harbour because most of the quays are reserved for commercial vessels, but there are some communal mooring buoys just W of the New Jetty.

If the rise of tide is enough you can cross the sill which dries *4·1m* into the Victoria marina where there are pontoons for visiting yachts. The Albert marina is reserved for local boats, and its sill dries *3·8m*. On page 21 is a table of depths over the marina sills; the depth inside is 1·58m minimum. Dinghies may land at a pontoon at the end of Victoria Pier. As a visiting yacht, you can't stay longer than 14 days without the Harbourmaster's permission. There are 2 most hospitable yacht clubs, the Royal Channel Islands and Guernsey Yacht Club, both marked on Chart G, p. 34A.

The North Beach marina has no facilities and is for local boats only. Two rectangular daytime marks at 270° take you 25m south of Reffée Card S buoy. The rear mark is an orange panel, the front red. A sectored light (Dir Occ WRG 10s) is centred on this same bearing. QkFl red and green pile lights form the final gateway. This is a sill marina with twin gates. Enter and exit always through the starboard side gate.

A fixed RED light indicates no entry or exit.

A fixed GREEN light indicates entry and exit permitted.

A fixed RED with a flashing AMBER indicates the gate has failed to open completely. Treat this as if the gates are closed.

A fixed GREEN with a flashing AMBER will be shown on the falling tide when the gates are about to close.

Fixed tide gauges show depth of water above closed gate level, i.e. Zero with gate in the upright position, which is 4.5m above Chart Datum. Auto Tide Gauge shows actual depth above gate in either closed or open position; it automatically adusts the displayed depth as gate open or closes. If one gate fails to open, the Auto Tide Gauge will indicate depth as if the gate is closed (in upright position).

5 – ST PETER PORT by the DUITE SAUVARY (5·0m)

Day: This is a useful short cut and apart from passing St Sampson entrance it avoids the NE flood stream in the Little Russel. First find yourself about half a mile SE of Platte Fougère light, chart F, p. 32A,

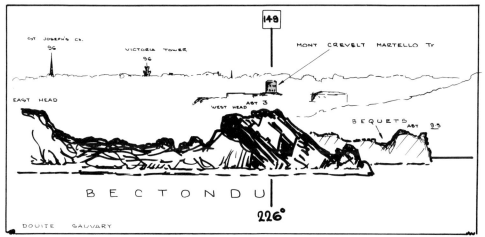

149 Mont Crevelt Martello Tower × the more western of 2 heads of Bectondu. When 50m from Bectondu, make a handrail eastabout of about 25m to clear both the rock and a *2·0m* head to its SW, until a stern mark is seen,

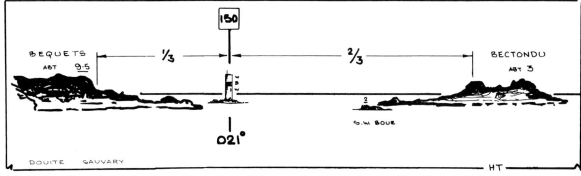

150 Platte Fougère Lt between Bequets and Bectondu, in the proportions shown. When abreast of Vivian you can come out into the Little Russel using the clearance mark **142** (207°) Castle Cornet white patch to the left of the Breakwater Lt, p. 96.

101

6 – ST SAMPSON from East (2·1m)

Day: When there is enough depth the approach is

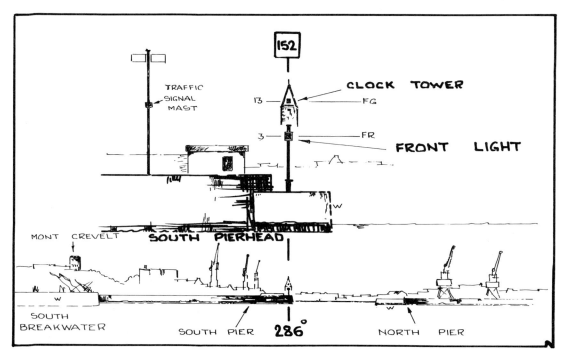

152 a clock tower × S pierhead (Chȃrt F, p. 32A).

Night: The same transit as above is used and for the final approach. The fixed red light in the middle of the harbour (Crocq Pier) must be seen through the pierheads. This is Guernsey's second harbour and is an official Port of Entry. Though a half-tide harbour it is the commercial centre of Guernsey and has the Channel Islands' only shipyard.

The harbour mouth dries *1·7m* and No 1 berth, on the stb'd hand on entering, dries *2·1m*. Berthing immediately to port after entry is prohibited above half tide. However, it has every possible facility except a yacht club. The Berthing Master, whose office is in the clock tower under the rear green leading light, will help find a berth for a yacht with legs. The shipyard on the N side has a patent slip for ships up to 55m × 12m. Buses run to Town every 10 minutes from a stop near the rear green leading light.

102

7 – BEAUCETTE MARINA and DOYLE PASSAGE (2.4m)

Day: Though not an official Port of Entry, Guernsey Customs make a concession for visiting yachtsmen and you can now clear inwards at Beaucette – the Channel Islands Yacht Marina – a private harbour. It is 3½ miles from Town, quiet and simple to enter. From line 149 take

154 Beaucette Marina leading marks. This transit leaves Petite Canupe buoy, black spar–'PC', a cable to stb'd (Chart F, p. 32A). The channel is between 5 red port and 5 green stb'd buoys, Priority of traffic is for entering yachts, and if the gauge on the N head, view 154, doesn't show enough water over the sill, there are 2 mooring buoys 100m outside. You are now out of the tide so anchoring outside is safe, hard sand, 6m. This is a sill marina and the entrance dries out *2·4m* but once in there is 20m minimum. Immediately inside, turn smartly to port to avoid a breakwater (made from old tyres) and use the pontoon marked 'Visitors'.

Night: Line 154 above is lit by 2 fixed red lights, shown 24 hours in summer.

A short-cut to the above transit from St Sampson is to come N by the Duite Sauvary, see p. 101, then cut the corner on

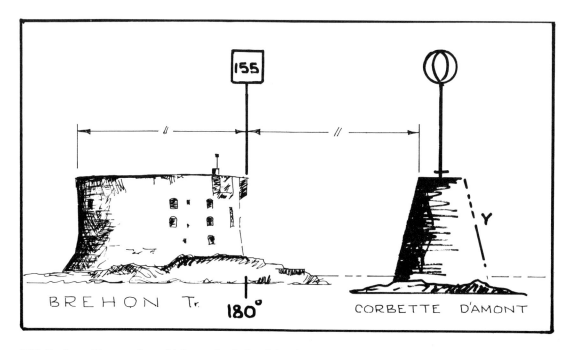

155 Brehon Tower, its width to the left of Corbette d'Amont Bn which joins line 154. Another most useful approach, this time from the NW, is by the Doyle Passage.

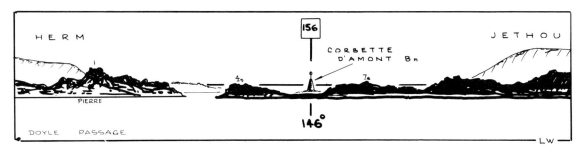

156 Corbette d'Amont midway between Herm and Jethou. Keep this beacon either in the middle or slightly toward Jethou as drawn. Fort Doyle is shown on view 154.

Beaucette, the first marina in the Channel Islands, has all facilities – water, electricity, showers, telephones, licenced restaurant, off-licence and food shop and fuel. It is ideal for leaving your yacht if you have to desert the islands without her. Buses run every 10 minutes to Town, but the stop is ½ mile distant. On page 21 is a table showing the depths over the sill. A daytime radio watch is kept on VHF Chan. 37.

There is unlimited car parking, and for slightly more than the price of this book you can have a car delivered alongside for a week's hire. There are 50 visitors' pontoon berths.

8 – ST SAMPSON from South (3·7m)

Day: This, the Coal Hole Passage, is the most direct route from Town to St Sampson and it starts S of Vivian Bn, view 131, p. 94.

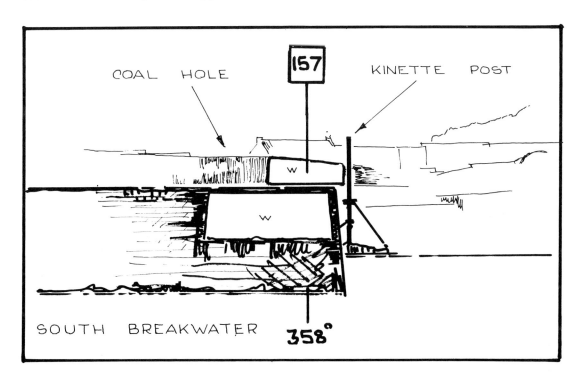

157 Two white patches in line. Going N, the patches can coincide as far as Vivian, but 1 ca. past, you must open them to the right until Kinette (a post on the shore under Vale Castle) just shows. When within 50m of the breakwater, circle it the same distance and enter the harbour (Chart F, p. 32A).

Night: Impossible.

9 – Round the Island

The pattern of Channel Islands cruises is only too often first to Cherbourg (to stock up with duty-free), to Alderney (to recover from The Race) and then to St Peter Port. After the delights of cheap booze have worn off, it's usually time to get back to the United Kingdom. So bestir yourself now, fill the tank and drink locker and come with me round the island. We will wait for fairly settled weather and, say, an hour after high water. Springs is the nicest time, when for most of the day the S and W coasts will be swell free and, in addition, going NE up the W coast the important stern marks will be in clear profile. We will start and finish at St Peter Port, going southabout.

The first bay S of Castle Cornet is Havelet and it offers a pleasant alternative to the crowded Town harbour. Leave Oyster Bn some 50m or so to stb'd, and enter the bay between this and Moulinet Bn, black with letter M.

105

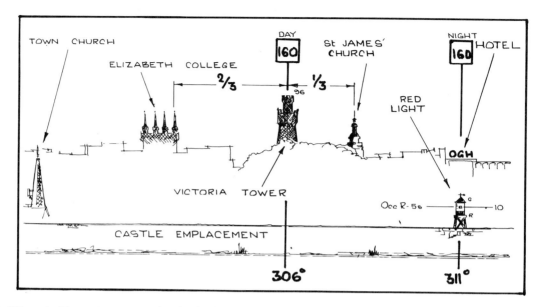

160 Victoria Tower between Elizabeth College and St James' Church (Chart G, p. 34A). On the same view, I show the night transit, the Old Government House Hotel illuminated sign × the red light on the marina entrance. When coming out of Havelet Bay and going southwards use

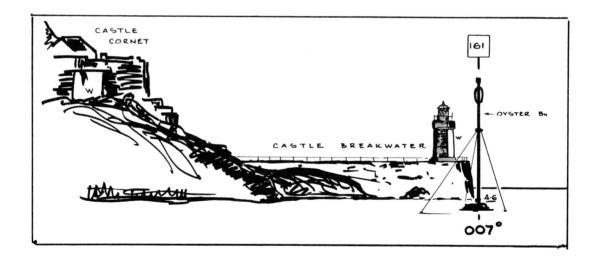

161 the breakwater light × Oyster Bn, which clears all the boues off Terres Point, until you can head into Soldiers' Bay (Chart H, p. 34A). Bec du Nez and Divette are 2 tiny bays for picnics, if you don't care for the tourist-oriented Fermain Bay. All this part of Guernsey is wooded and green, with steep cliffs. Scores of people have hit Gabrielle Rock (*1·6m*) but the eastern clearance is

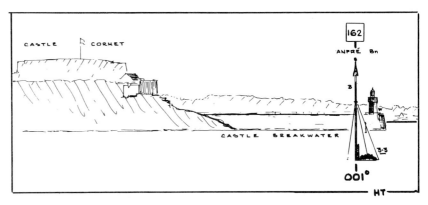

162 Breakwater Lt × Anfré Bn. For the inside clearance use

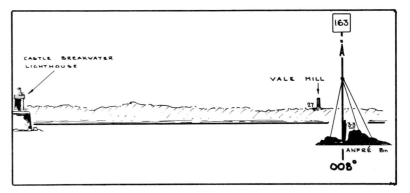

163 Vale Mill × Anfré Bn. Perhaps because it is so near the picnic bays, Gabrielle has now been awarded a set of Bns as striking marks.

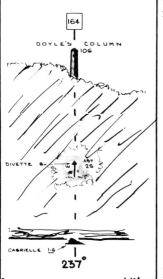

164 Doyle's Column × Divette Bn. The other is

107

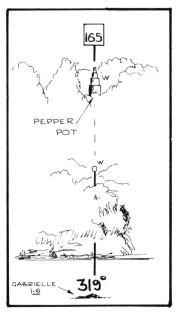

165 Fermain Pepper Pot × a white Bn.
To round St Martin's Point, give an offing of 1ca. round Longue Pierre and take

170 Brehon Tower to the right of Longue Pierre Bn, which clears to the E of the Grunes de Jobourg.

Now come the 6 miles of the S coast, most of which is deep close in. It forms an impressive line of cliffs, fortunately devoid of houses, in which are many lovely bays. Not all are as uncomfortable on the high water as you might suppose; all are quiet from half-tide down. The 3 key marks are 2 German towers, view 131, and the Hanois LtHo; all are quite unmistakable and can't possibly be confused with each other.

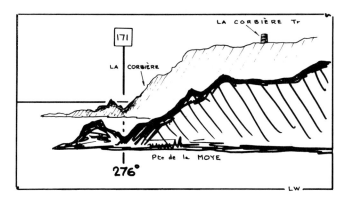

171 The 'V' of Corbière × the 'V' of Pointe de la Moye clear to the S of the Grunes de Jerbourg. Now you can explore Petit Port, Moulin Huet and Saints Bay, all sandy and easy to find.

If the tide rises enough to clear the 1·9m boue, you may continue on line 171, which takes you between Baleine and Icart Point. Alternatively, when Icart Point bears N, turn on to

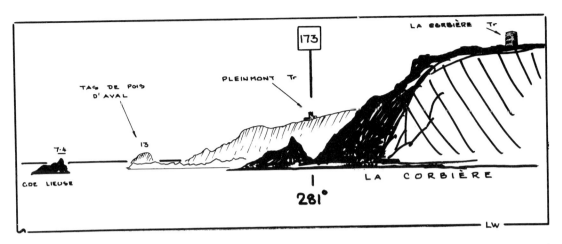

173 Pleinmont Tower × the 'V' of Corbière. Here there are 3 more anchorages: Icart Bay, Petit Bôt and le Gouffre (Chart I, p. 36A).

Turn now to seaward to avoid Rousse (<u>6·7m</u>),

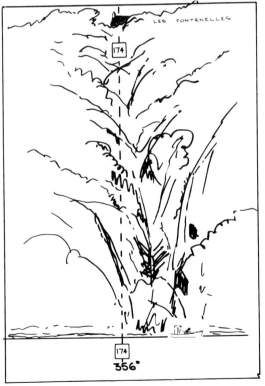

174 les Fontenelles × the valley below, and continue westwards along

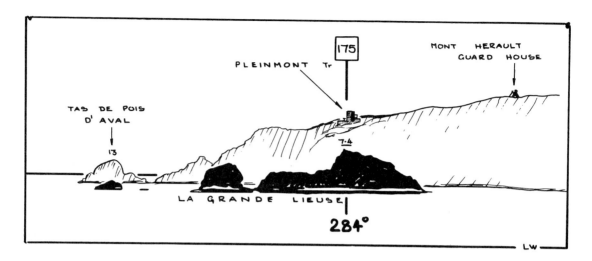

175 Pleinmont Tower × la Grande Lieuse, a seldom-covered rock below la Corbière. Now you have 2 choices: to clear off into the ocean or to keep close in. The easy one comes first. When 1ca. off la Grande Lieuse,

176 a house × the valley below. This white house, La Roche, is one of the very few visible on this stretch of coast.

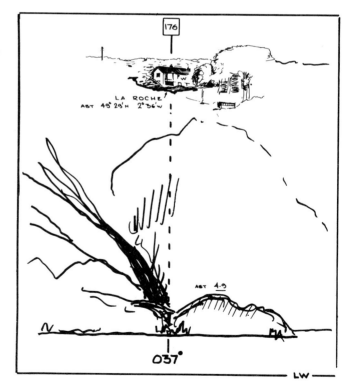

110

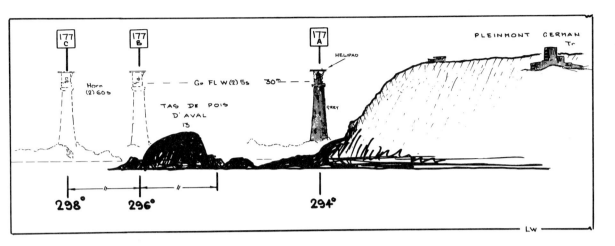

177A les Hanois LtHo touching the cliff below Pleinmont Tower. You need be quite sober when looking at 177: my 3 lighthouses are drawn together for convenience. When the Corbière Tower bears NE it's time to come outside again to clear les Kaines d'Amont on **177B** (296°) les Hanois LtHo just outside Tas de Pois d'Aval (Chart J, p. 36A). Now let's go back to where the frightened navigators peeled off, near la Corbière, and take the inshore passage. This is easier at low water when the rocks are showing, and after rounding Grande Lieuse 20m to the South, look over your shoulder and you should see

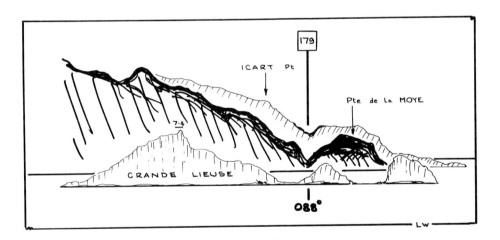

179 the 'V' of Icart Point × the 'V' of Pointe de la Moye (Chart I, p. 36A). Turn N when the Corbière Tower bears NE and take

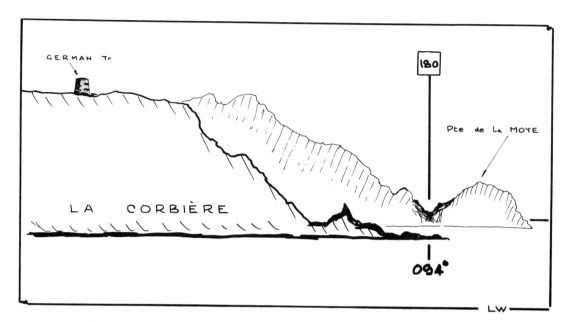

180 the 'V' of Pointe de la Moye × la Corbière. Lines 180 and 177B join Chart J, p. 36A, at

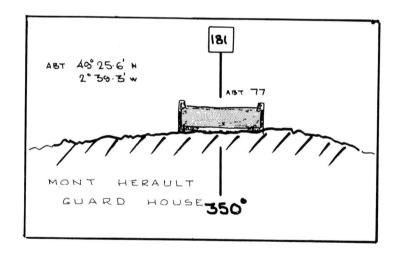

181 Mount Herault guardhouse, with neither gable showing. Out again, and the last time we use les Hanois. **177C** (298°) les Hanois LtHo open to the left of Tas de Pois d'Aval.

Now we are ready to round the SW tip of Guernsey, but just before doing so try Gull Bay for a summer's afternoon anchorage. The easiest entrance, with a hand rock-dodging for'd, is from the SE, between Tas de Pois d'Aval and the cliff.

Don't pass too close to the S of this 13m rock, some boues lie ½ ca. to its S, and W. Next the W coast marks, but first make sure of your position (Chart J, p. 36A) by

112

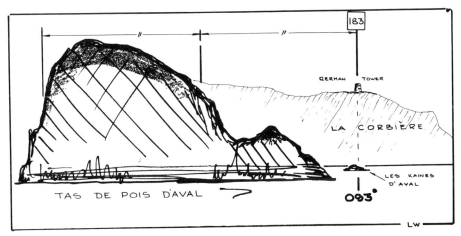

183 la Corbière Tower to the right of Tas de Pois d'Aval and as a check

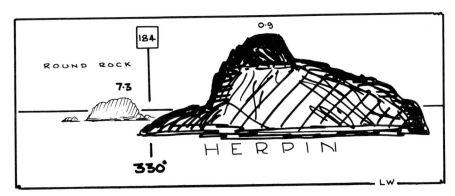

184 Round Rock × Herpin: both transits clear inside Bassière (1·8m). The 2-mile square of rocks on the SW of Guernsey is dominated by les Hanois LtHo and a big central rock called the Round Rock. All the channels are between 8m and 15m deep, and it isn't a good place to be above half tide; not only is the swell of the flood a serious thing, but the rocks start covering and in no time you are lost. However, this is no time for philosophising, so take

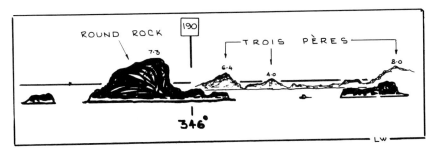

190 the W head of les Trois Pères to the right of Round Rock (Chart K, p. 38A). Two ca. short of the rock come to stb'd on

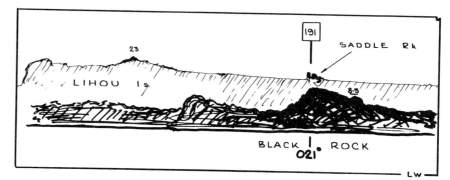

191 the Saddle Rock on Lihou Island × E head of Black Rock.

It's about time for a break, or even a night stop, so let's try Portelet. The mark for the turn is

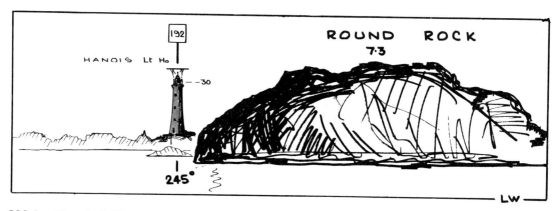

192 les Hanois LtHo to the left of Round Rock. Come eastwards on

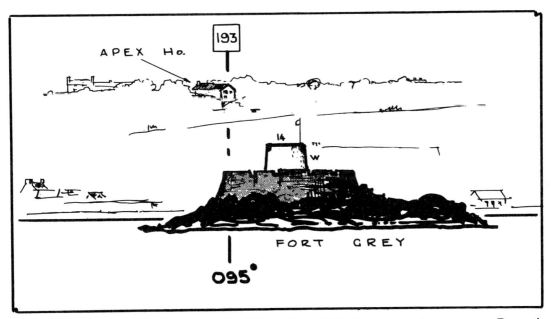

193 Apex House × the left-hand wall of Fort Grey. This fort used to be known as Roquaine Castle, but I prefer the local name 'Cup and Saucer': it has recently been restored and made into a fine maritime museum. After ¾ mile along transit 193, the tiny stone quay can be seen and you can either anchor when the final mark comes on or go in and dry out.

194 Trinity House Cottage × the post on la Varde quay.

Back now to **191** (021°) Saddle Rock on Lihou × E head of Black Rock, after which you come to a small stb'd turn on to

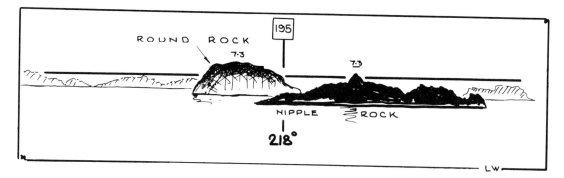

195 Round Rock to the left of Nipple Rock, the breast mark for this turn being

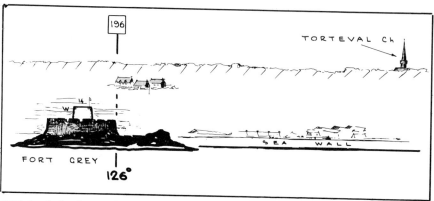

196 the left of a small cluster of houses × the right wall of Fort Grey. Three ca. later a sharp port turn,

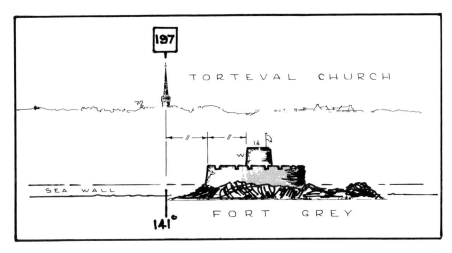

197 Torteval Church × Fort Grey. If held exactly as shown, this clears NE of Black Rock and the _3·4m_ boue, but it will take you too close to Fourquie. Since this dries _5·8m_ and is perpendicular on its SW face and will be showing, make a dog leg to the SW until past, as shown (Chart K, p. 38A). This mark takes you right out to sea (Chart Y, p. 32A).

You now have a right-angled stb'd turn followed by ¾ mile without marks; however, since it would be stupid to be dodging around this corner above half tide, you can leave the Corner Rock and la Pècheresse a good 1ca. to stb'd on a course of 055°. Turn towards the shore on

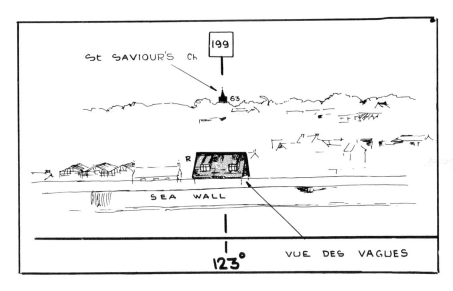

199 St Saviour's Church × house, 'Vue des Vagues'. This isolated red-roofed house is on the coast road and leads to an anchorage in the bight NE of Lihou. This island is privately owned but visitors are welcomed. Benedictine monks from Mont St Michel, France, built a priory on Lihou in A.D. 1114 and the ruins still remain.

117

Continue NE up the coast on

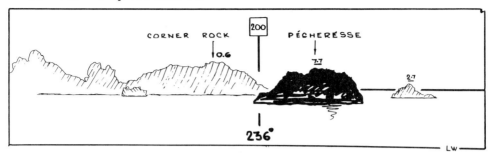

200 Corner Rock × la Pècheresse. I've drawn these offset for clarity, but the 2 peaks should coincide. Note in the same view the small *2·7m* boue midway between those 2 rocks.

The next milestone is the Black Moulière over 2 miles distant where you must perform a small dog-leg (Chart L, p. 38A).

201 Fort Hommet to the right of Black Moulière shows us when to turn about ESE and

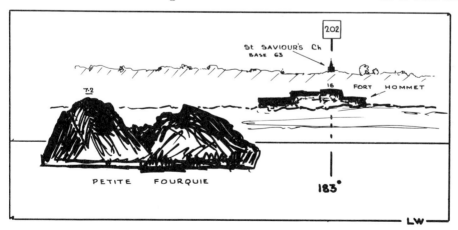

202 St Saviour's Church × Fort Hommet gives you the hint to continue on

118

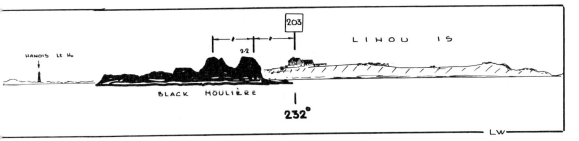

203 the E house on Lihou Island open to the right of Black Moulière. Make sure of this mark: you'll need it for another 2 miles. You will pass 5 bays here: Perelle, Vazon, Cobo, Saline and Portinfer: All are shallow, unsheltered, encumbered with rocks and best explored in sea-boots with bucket and spade.

We are now coming to an area dominated by Martello towers. They are numbered from 4 to 11 on Chart M, p. 40A. (somebody must have made off with number 8). One is now used as a back-door entrance to Grande Havre.

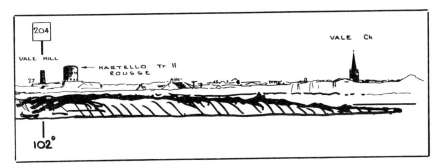

204 Vale Mill to the left of Martello tower No. 11. The second mark will take you across the Col du Pont (*3·7m*)

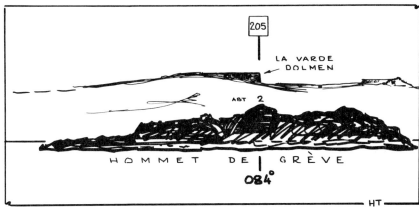

205 a dolmen near la Varde × Hommet de Grève. Should you instead, however, want to clear out to sea, there is an excellent mark just N of l'Étac,

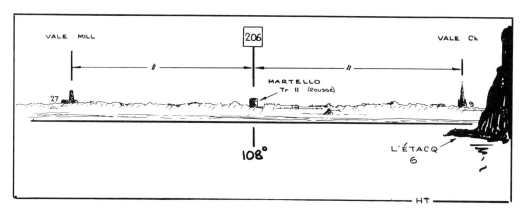

206. Martello tower No. 11, midway between Vale Mill and Vale Church (Chart Y, p. 32A). Still on line 203, we come to a rather tricky dogleg, Platte Fougère being the key.

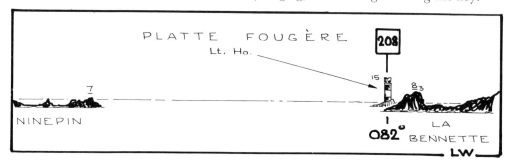

208 Platte Fougère × la Bennette. This leads 25m south of Quenon (*7.7m*). Half a mile along this mark there are 3 choices: carry on eastwards, take to the open sea, or turn S to Grand Havre. The last 2 have a common mark

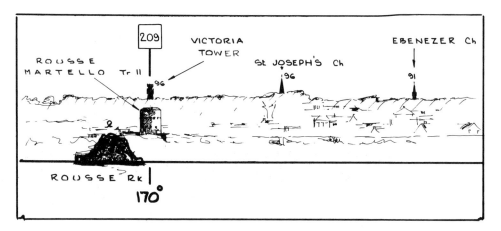

209 Victoria Tower × Martello Tower No. 11 (Chart Y, p. 32A). Why not spend a night in Grand Havre? Turn E on

210 Chouet Tower × a German bunker. This tower may be removed as it interferes with a quarry, but a course of 090° on the bunker is safe. Enter the harbour on

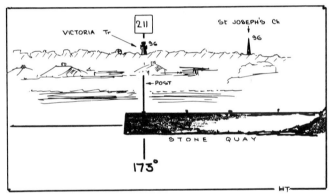

211 Victoria Tower × the end of the quay. Grand Havre is a useful anchorage and fishing harbour, and has a pub or two, an hotel and grocery shops. Buses to Town frequently. The 130m-long stone quay has steps at the end where there is 2·7m at half tide—i.e. it dries *2·3m*.

The top is awash at the same moment.

To carry on eastwards, the lower the tide the better.

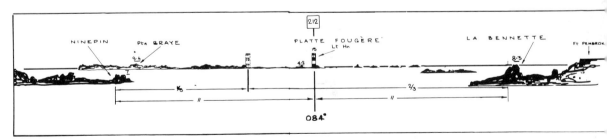

212 Platte Fougère midway between Ninepin Rock and la Bennette. When abreast of Fort Pembroke borrow slightly to the N to put Platte Fougère in the position shown. About here you can take a diversion to a fine sandy bay, l'Ancresse,

121

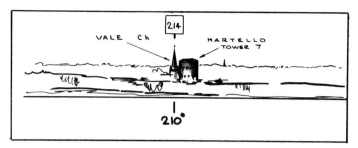

214 Vale Church × Martello tower No. 7. After this **156** (146°) Corbette d'Amont between Herm and Jethou, p. 104, takes us to the Beaucette marina, or alternatively you can go back to Town (Chart Y, p. 32A).

The rest of the trip down to St Sampson has been described and there are only 2 tiny harbours left. Just over 1ca. S of Bequets on the Duite Sauvary the entrance to Bordeaux is seen (Chart F, p. 32A).

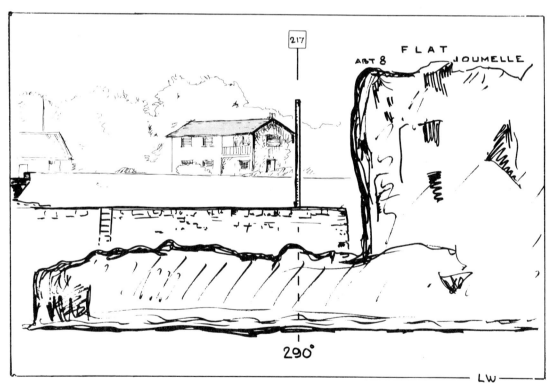

217 Gable of a house and the post on the quay just to the left of Flat Joumelle. Thread your way in between fishing boats or anchor outside. Bordeaux has a 10-minute bus service to Town and a grocery shop. The quay below the post dries at half tide and the end of the SE quay dries at low water.

There is another tiny harbour, la Salerie, about half a mile north of St Peter Port. It's worth exploring and there are shops, etc., nearby without going into Town. The entrance is

220 a conical roof × the end of the quay. The harbour dries out about half tide but you can anchor S of the Quaine Bn where shown on Chart G, p. 34A. There are buses every few minutes to Town.

5 Jersey

Here is the biggest, richest, most populated of all the islands. It has more millionaires, traffic jams and luxury hotels than the rest of the Channel Islands together. But also there are friendly people and beautiful country, uncrowded anchorages and miniature harbours around the coast. Don't judge Jersey by St Helier and, if you want a quiet time, don't spend longer there than it takes to clear your boat inwards.

There's a patois saying specially suitable for St Helier harbour – *'p'tit patchet, long ch'min coûte.* It's a poky little thing resulting from lack of foresight of our great-great-grandfathers. Here you will be trampled underfoot by cargo steamers, mail boats, car ferries and hydrofoils. The harbour staff are wonderfully helpful to visiting yachtsmen.

To repeat what you read earlier, you must only enter Jersey at St Helier or Gorey. Heavy penalties enough to knock you flat are most readily available from the States if you fail to do this, so the main approach leading lines given here aim for these harbours. Fortunately Jersey coasts are well lit and beautifully marked by first-class beacons which are carefully maintained – a credit to the States of Jersey Harbours and Airports Committee who alone are responsible for all the navigational aids. Of the 30 buoys in the Channel Islands only 5 are outside Jersey waters.

As with all the islands, the tides are there to be used and from the tidal diagrams you will see that Jersey, which is roughly rectangular, has a regular pattern of tidal currents. When it is slack water E and W, the current is maximum on the N and S coasts, and roughly vice versa. So if you approach from the direction of Guernsey, try to be at the NW corner, Grosnez, at half-tide down so that fair tide takes you for nine hours up to Town. If coming from Alderney or Guernsey and bound for Gorey via St Catherine, try and find yourself on the N coast around low water. Then favourable current will allow you 4 hours for the job. Coming N from St Malo via the E of les Minquiers, nearly 7 hours of fair tide can be used; depart St Malo an hour before high water so as to arrive near St Helier at low water.

There are umpteen approaches you can make if you study the Admiralty charts but when nearing the island there are 10 transits – 8 to St Helier, 2 to Gorey – which are shown on Chart Z, p. 42A. How much to depart from these transits is easily seen from a quick glance at the coastal Charts N, R and Q.

* 'a small thing gets to be a burden in the long run'

1 – ST HELIER, North-west Passage (8·5m)

Day: The approach from Guernsey is straightforward and it is only a matter of avoiding the dangers in St Ouen's Bay. The first is off Grosnez Point, Chart Z, p. 42A.

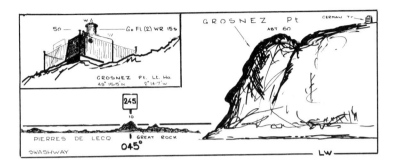

245 The highest rock of the Pierres de Lecq to the left of Grosnez Point – Swashway Channel – which clears the boues off Étac. If you wish to tack into St Ouen's Bay

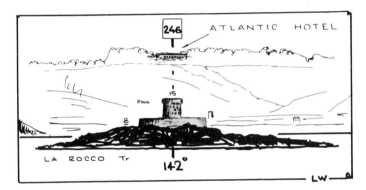

246 the Atlantic Hotel × la Rocco Tower is the clearance mark. Don't go nearer than half a mile from the tower. Turn SW

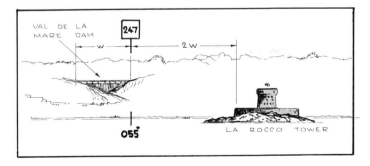

247 Val de la Mare Dam well to the left of Rocco Tower, which clears the rocks off la Corbière (Chart N, p. 44A); ¾ mile must be given from the LtHo on the NW and W. Turn southwards until you can see

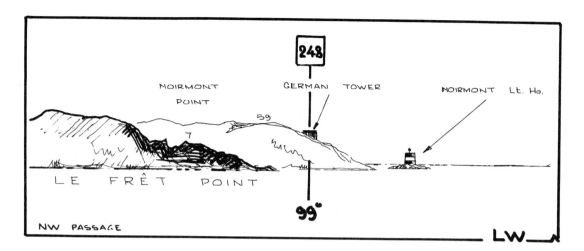

248 the German tower on Noirmont Point to the right of le Frêt Point. Carry on eastwards until

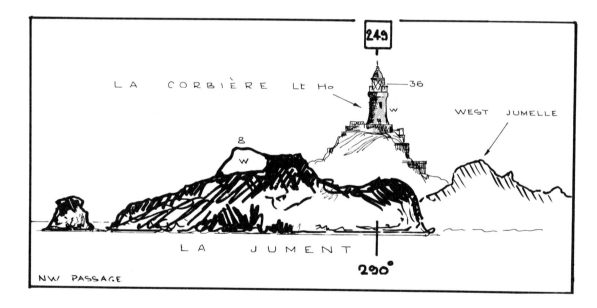

249 la Corbière LtHo to the right of la Jument, which is painted white. Just before coming abreast of Noirmont Point, take the Western passage (see p. 127).

Night: The white sector of Grosnez Lt clears the N end of St Ouen's Bay. Come S, keeping in the white sector of la Corbière Lt: when the fixed red (on the shore) and la Corbière Lt come in line (079°) it is time to locate the Ruaudière buoy to the right of Noirmont Lt. Follow this for about 3 miles across St Brelade's Bay until la Corbière Lt touches la Moye Point, which leads into the Western lighted passage. The last 2 night transits are almost the same as lines 248 and 249.

2 – ST HELIER, Western Passage (4·0m)

Day: The main transit coming in from the W is

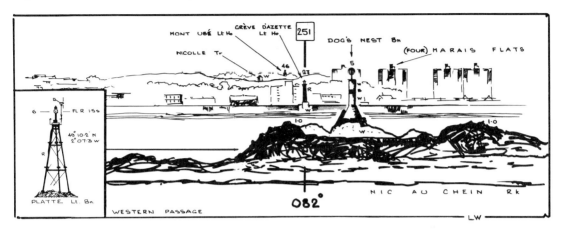

251 Grève d'Azette LtHo × Dog's Nest Bn. This transit passes over Passage Rock (4·0m) but if you borrow to the N to leave the Passage Rock buoy on your stb'd hand the whole channel then carries 6 metres.

Night: The same transit is used, but since the Dog's Nest Bn isn't lit, the mark becomes Mont Ubé Lt in line with Grève d'Azette Lt. Mont Ubé only just shows above the trees so is almost invisible except at night.

3 – ST HELIER, Danger Rock Passage (5·8m)

Day: This is a tributary of the Western passage and the mark must be kept exactly as shown,

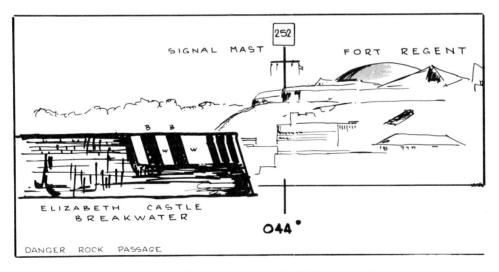

252 the signal mast at Fort Regent × the end of Elizabeth Castle breakwater.

Night: Unlit: use the Red and Green passage, p. 129.

127

4 – ST HELIER, Sillette Passage (6·1m)

Day: These are the marks for coming up from the S if you want to go to St Aubin. Since you can't enter your boat there without first clearing at St Helier, they are mostly used for departing, not arriving. However, going northwards, take

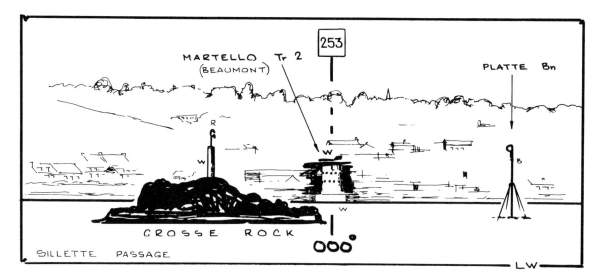

253 Martello tower No. 2 × the right side of Grosse Rock.
   Night: Unlit: use the Red and Green passage, p. 129.

5 – ST HELIER, South Passage (8·0m)

Day: A very conspicuous mark coming up from the S, and which joins the Red and Green passage, p. 129, is

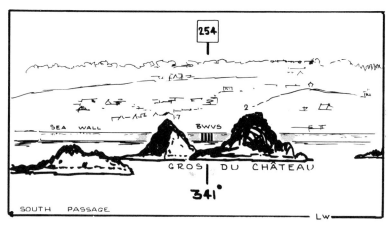

254 the black-and-white vertical stripes on the sea-wall between the twin heads of Gros du Château.
   Night: Unlit: use the Eastern passage, p. 129, instead

6 – ST HELIER, 'Electric' Passage (9.8m)

Day: This isn't really a passage at all and the Harbour Committee has not even given it a name. It uses as a far mark a giant chimney 95m high carrying boiler and engine exhausts from the power station. So if you agree on the name, put this erection

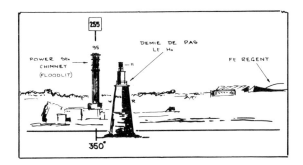

255 Power Station chimney × Demi de Pas Lt. When 2½ca. south of the Demi de Pas Lt. turn to port along the Eastern Passage (7 below).

Night: Since the chimney is floodlit, the same transit can be used.

7 – ST HELIER, Eastern Passage (7.0m)

Day: No daytime marks can be given for this very broad route, which joins the Red and Green passage, p. 129 (Chart R, p. 48A). On a course of 314° the Demi de Pas Lt should be left 1½ca. to stb'd, the Hinguette buoy 2ca. to port until the marks for the Red and Green passage appear.

Night: Pass W of Demi de Pas Lt (as by day) and when abeam, steer 314° for the red isophase Lt on St Aubin's pierhead. After passing the Hinguette buoy, alter course to port to bring Noirmont Point Lt on the Ruaudière buoy (280°) until the Red and Green leading lights are seen.

8 – ST HELIER, Red and Green Passage (2.7m) and harbour entrance

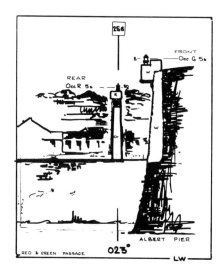

Day: All the previous passages join this, which unfortunately passes over Fairway Rock (1.2m) (Chart N, p. 44A), so study your tide tables and exercise caution as to when it is safe to use the southern part of this passage.

The Red and Green Passage has been cleared to 2.5m for 80m either side of the leading line between 49°09.9′N and 49°10.3′N.

256 Orange and white daymarks in line.
Night: The same transit is used, the lights being synchronized.
Note: This diagram was prepared before completion of the Ferry Terminal: see Chart S, p. 42A.

The rest of the entrance is on Chart S, p. 42A. Two fixed green lights (078°) lead you through the 1ca.-wide entrance, where there is the Port Control office with traffic signals on the roof and sides. You will be told by loudhailer or Channel 14 where to berth.

St Helier Port Control Signals

Signal	Meaning
FG or FlG	Entry only
FR or FlR	Exit only
Any G or R together	Exit or entry stopped
Any of the above + QkFl Amber	*Power boats under 25m long may enter or leave at their own risk.

*This does not include yachts under sail. If you are foolish enough to try and enter under sail the control officer will treat you like a big steamer.

La Collette Basin is a waiting area and has visitors' berths. If there is a space and enough tide rise in the St Helier Marina, Port Control will direct you to enter via the commercial harbour. The marina has an automatic sill-gate shown on Fig 9.

The time between the sill-gate starting to close and reaching the upright position varies with neaps and springs. However, in the interests of safety, no attempt should be made to enter or depart when the red light – flashing or fixed – is exhibited. In its closed position, the top of the sill-gate is at a height of tide of 5·0m above chart datum (1·4m on the Marina Entrance Depth Indicator Board). When the sill-gate is in the open position, a green light is exhibited on the Marina cross-wall. On a falling tide, the red indicator light commences flashing at a height of tide of 5·8m above chart datum (2·2m on the Marina Entrance Depth Indicator Board). The red light (which after a short period of flashing becomes fixed) denotes that the sill-gate has moved to the closed position. Both St Helier Marina and la Collette have all the usual facilities.

It is just over 2 miles across to St Aubin, a drying harbour to the NW, to be described later, and once entered at St Helier or Gorey you can depart from anywhere around Jersey. Simply fill in the Notice of Sailing they will hand you on entering, and drop it in any letter box before leaving.

Fig. 9. St Helier Marina automatic sill-gate

9 – GOREY from the South-east with entrance (3·4m)

There are only 2 more approach transits, both for Gorey, to describe. This harbour dries _5m_ at the outer part and not only is it well sheltered from prevailing winds, but nearest to France and Alderney. The same entry regulations apply as in Town, but there are no traffic lights.

Day: This mark, if it can be detected so far, can start 10 miles to the SE (Chart Z, p. 42A).

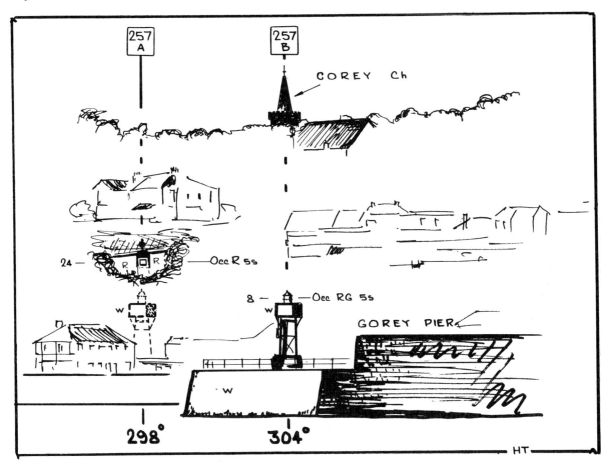

257B Gorey Church × the white patch at the end of the pier (Chart Q, p. 46A).

Night: The 2 leading lights, line **257A**, are powerful, both 12-mile range, and are almost the same as the daytime transit, line **257B**, and clear everything. It is interesting to note, by the way, that the red/green sector cut-off is the same bearing, 304°, as a transit 257B.

Gorey is a large village and a port of entry. On the pier are fuel, water from a hose, telephone, Harbour and Customs Offices, besides toilets and Gorey Yacht Club. Buses are every 20 minutes to Town, taking half an hour.

10 – GOREY from North-east (6·1m)

Day: Approaching from Carteret or from les Écrehou, the transit can be taken from 6 miles off

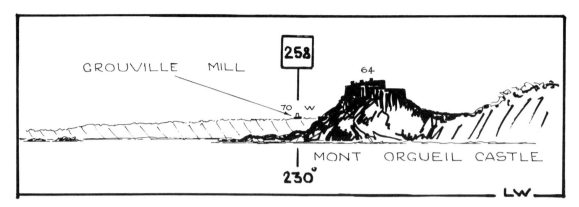

258 Grouville Mill × the S face of Mont Orgeuil Castle. The mill has a white top and has been converted into a house. When ¾ mile off the castle, turn sharply to port,

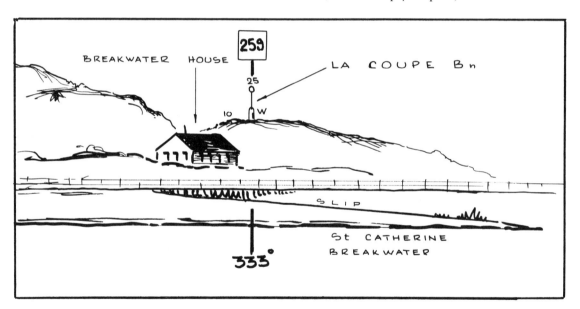

259 la Coupe Bn just to the right of Breakwater House on Verclut Point. Though this mark need only be followed for 3ca. in order to enter Gorey, it can also be used for the Violet channel, p. 138. In fact, given enough visibility you can follow it towards Granville (see my *French Pilot, Vol. 1*, line 4B).

The final mark that passes 100m to the S of les Arch Bn is

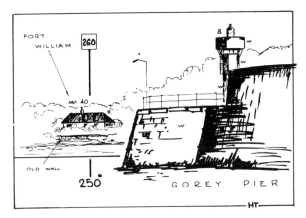

260 Fort William × the end of Gorey pier. The back mark is ill-named for it is a modern red-roofed house built on top of the remains of the old fort.

Night: Useless, try

257A (298°) Gorey leading lights, p. 131.

11 – ST HELIER to GOREY, Gument Passage (7·0m)

Day: This is the most thrilling, the shortest, the most interesting passage in Jersey. Locally known as the 'gutters', it carries – providing you don't wander more than a few yards from the marks - one metre with an 8m rise of tide. Therefore a yacht drawing, say, 1·5m (5ft) wouldn't feel safe with much less than a 10·5m tide. So set out from Town about an hour before high water, making sure you have an anchor handy, the engine has enough fuel, and your helmsman has strong nerves. Needless to add, good visibility and no swell are essential; so, with those pubs in Gorey a-beckoning, here we go. *Si vous r'viraïz, caöntaïz dix* – If you think it time to turn back, first count ten. (Chart R, p. 48A).

Steam out of St Helier harbour on the now familiar **256** (023°) Red and Green passage daymarks, p. 129. Turn E on

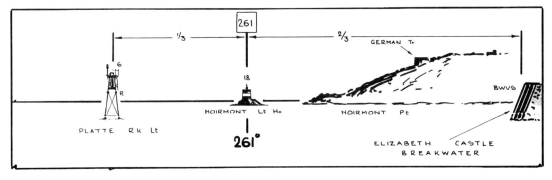

261 Noirmont LtHo between Platte Rock Lt and Elizabeth Castle breakwater. Skirt the sea-wall 20m off until you can see above it

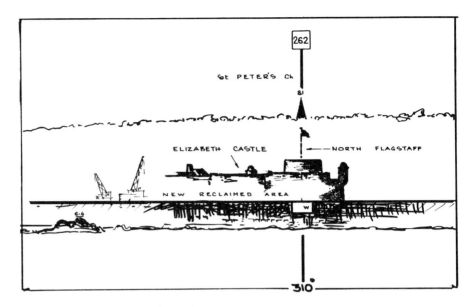

262 St Peter's Church spire × a white patch on the harbour wall. After a mile, look fine to port for a breast mark,

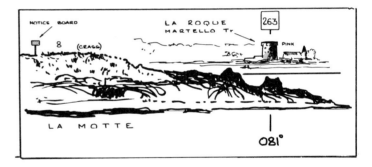

263 la Roque Martello tower to the right of la Motte Point. This signals a turn on to the stern mark,

264 the Flat Rock between Noirmont Lt and Noirmont German tower. Here is where, if you think you've had enough, you can chicken out to the wide ocean on

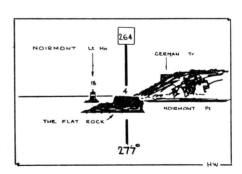

265 le Hocq Martello tower × the SE head of la Motte. This leaves the Round Rouget Rock a barnacle's thickness to port and the Demi de Pas Lt ½ca. to stb'd.

However, continuing along line 264, look out for a stern mark

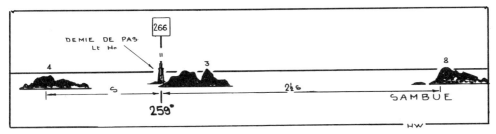

266 Demi de Pas Lt to the left of a 3·0m-high rock just S of la Sambue. To locate this rather important point, here are not one but 2 breast marks. The first is

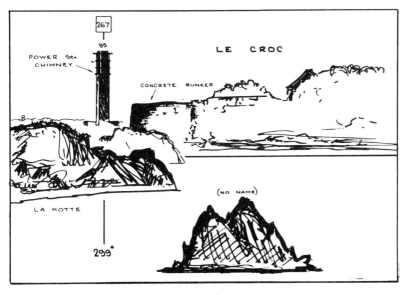

267 the power station chimney × a German bunker at le Croc. The second is

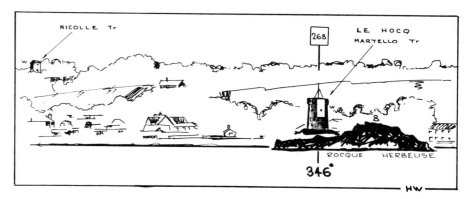

268 le Hocq Martello tower × Roque Herbeuse. After about a mile comes an important transit,

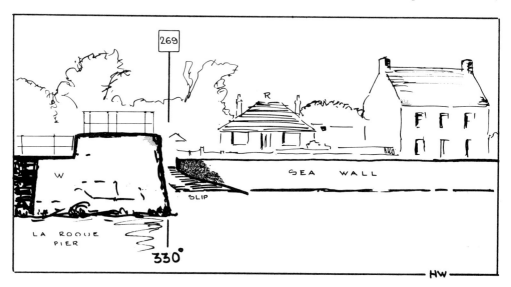

269 the slip at la Roque × the end of the pier. Here is your second chance for the open sea, for this line takes you SE towards the Violet channel. First, however, there is a breast mark,

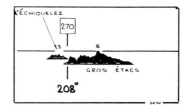

270 l'Échiquelez × Gros Étacs. Line 269 takes you in to la Roque. Dodge E of the pier and find a vacant spot among the fishing boats, ship your legs and relax. This is a charming, snug harbour in fine weather with few facilities except a shop or so, and a bus to Town every 20 minutes, taking 20 minutes.

Leaving la Roque to continue northwards

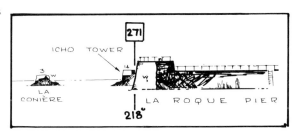

271 Icho Tower just peeping round the end of la Roque pier. The final exit which joins line 270 is

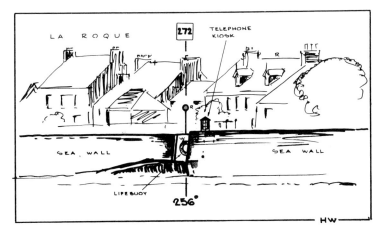

272 a small red daymark × the sea-wall. From this junction there is only one mark and it's 2 miles away to the N.

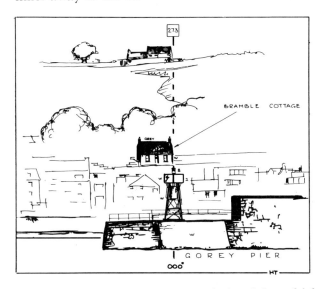

273 Bramble Cottage × Gorey pierhead Lt, which takes you right across Grouville Bay, to Gorey (Chart Q, p. 46A).
   Night: Unlit.

137

12 – ST HELIER to GOREY, Violet channel (9·0m)

Day: This is the big-ship route from Town to Gorey, so leave on

256 (023°) Red and Green channel daymarks, p. 129. When past East Rock buoy take the S passage, **254** (341°) black-and-white vertical stripes on the sea-wall between the twin heads of Gros du Château, p. 128. When about 3ca. north of Hinguette buoy follow the reciprocal of the Eastern Passage, p. 129; i.e. on a course of 134° steer so as to leave the Demi de Pas Lt 1½ca. to port. When the Electric Passage transit shows up (Line 255 p. 129) and also you are some 2½ca. south of the light, steer east and take a stern mark

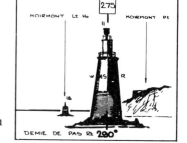

275 Noirmont LtHo to the left of Demi de Pas Lt. When you come to the breast mark

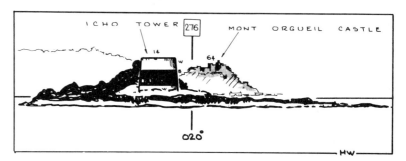

276 Mont Orgueil Castle to the right of Icho Tower you are in la Route en Ville, Chart R, p. 48A. Leave la Conchière 2ca. to port and position yourself at an important 'crossroad', for which there are 2 marks,

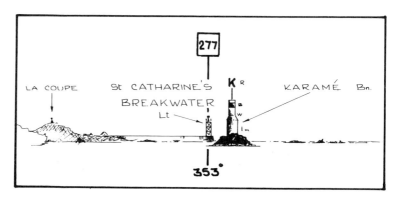

277 St Catherine's breakwater Lt × Karamé Bn and

138

278 Icho Tower to the left of la Conchière. This last Bn is deliberately bent towards N. Use this last line as a stern mark until the Violet channel buoy bears NE. The buoy, which is a 'safe-water' buoy, can be used as a turning point: it is clear ¾ mile all round (Chart Z, p. 42A). When about ¾ mile N of the buoy, locate **259** (333°) la Coupe Bn × Breakwater House, p. 132. If you look eastwards, the 2 Anquette Bns (101° – shown on Chart Z) help. After nearly 3 miles you will come on to **257B** (304°) Gorey Church × the white patch at the end of the pier to enter Gorey harbour, p. 131.

Night: Possible but only for powerful swimmers.

13 – ST HELIER to GOREY, Brett Passage (1·0m)

Day: This is the best small-boat, power or sail, route. Except for a small part by Brett Bn, it carries nearly 3m throughout, but as the best time to start from Town is about 2 hours before high water, this should not bother you. Take the marks for the Violet channel, p. 138, as far as the 'crossroads', where lines 277 and 278 intersect (Chart R, p. 48A). From here, steer 027° so as to leave Brett Bn 20–30m on your stb'd hand. This is the shallowest part. A course of 005° leaves le Cochon buoy just to port until

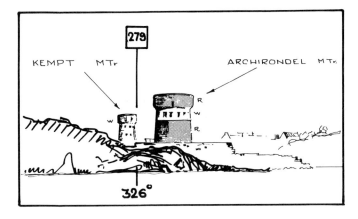

279 Kempt Martello tower just to the left of Archirondel Martello tower, which joins **257B** (304°) Gorey Church × the white patch at the end of the pier to enter Gorey harbour, p. 131.

Night: Hopeless. Take a bus.

14 – ST HELIER to GOREY, St Clement Anchorages

You may have noticed during the Gument passage some tiny anchorages on the S coast, so here are the marks, in order from W – E (Chart R, p. 48A).

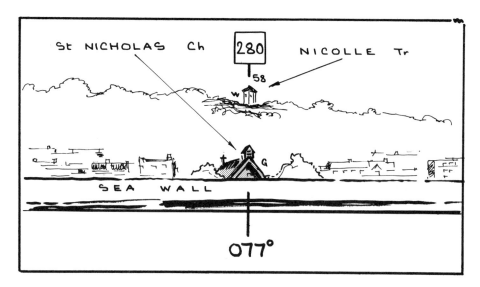

280 Nicolle Tower × St Nicholas Church. This and the next are near to handy launching slips at Grève d'Azette.

281 Marais Flat (the nearest of 4) × a slate-roofed house. The next anchorage is le Croc.

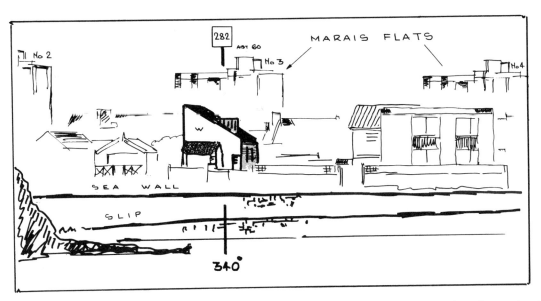

282 Marais Flat No. 3 (counting from seaward) × a prominent wedge-shaped roof near the slip. With legs this is a snug little sandy cove: it dries about _8·9m_.
Now we come to le Hocq,

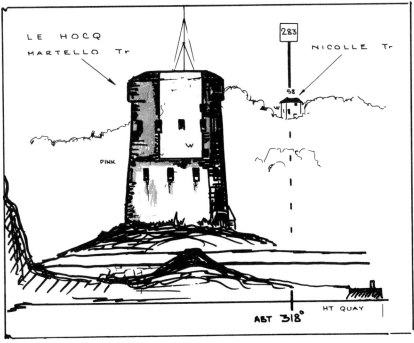

283 Nicolle Tower to the right of le Hocq Martello tower. When within 2ca. of the tower come slightly eastwards on

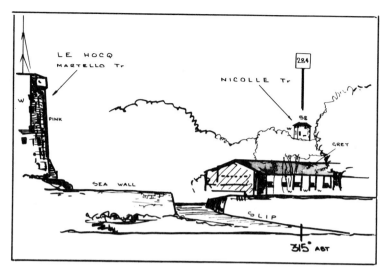

284 Nicolle Tower × St Clement's parish hall. This is another snug place with legs. The bottom is sand and there is a tiny low-water pier of stone. It dries out about *9·0m*.

15 – GOREY to ST HELIER (Northabout)

It is time now to continue our trip around the island. Tides aren't all that important, though inspection of the tidal charts, pp. 20, 21, will show that high-water is the best starting time for going N from Gorey. Quit by the NE entrance, p. 132, and leave le Fara Bn lca. to port, Chart Q, p. 46A. Ann Port, Archirondel and St Catherine are 3 charming, partially drying anchorages for which no marks are needed – simple bearings on 2 Martello towers are safe. St Catherine has a sailing club, a shop, a pub and a bus service to town, but the breakwater is foul throughout its length. Round the end of St Catherine's breakwater, noting the 0·9m rock (Pillon) 1½ca. off the end, and look for 2 clearance marks,

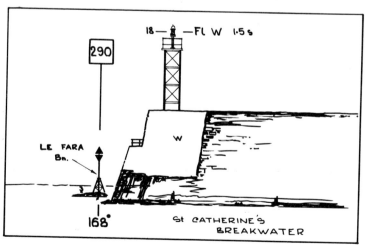

290 le Fara Bn × white patch on breakwater and

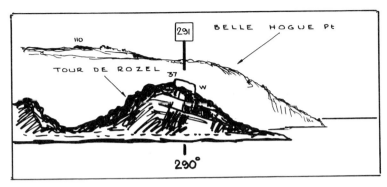

291 Belle Hogue Point × the white mark on Tour de Rozel, which brings you into Rozel bay. Allow 2ca. off Nez de Guet and Tour de Rozel and you are into Bouley Bay (Chart P, p. 50A) and on

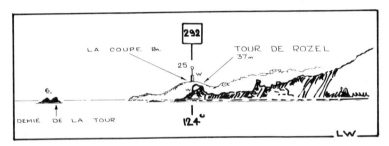

292 la Coupe Bn × Tour de Rozel white mark.

But aren't you missing 2 lovely little harbours? For Rozel put

293 a cartwheel on a restaurant 'The Granite Corner' × the pierhead. The directional light shows a 2° white sector. The pier dries about _1·3m._ Rozel has a shop, a pub and an hourly bus to Town (30 minutes).

To clear les Troupeurs into Bouley Bay, put

294 right side of Fort Lester × the white pier end. Unlit, Bouley harbour dries $\overline{1\cdot6m}$ and possesses a hotel, a pub, a nearby shop and buses to Town (30 minutes). Rejoin line

292 (124°), la Coupe Bn × Tour de Rozel white mark, p. 143, using

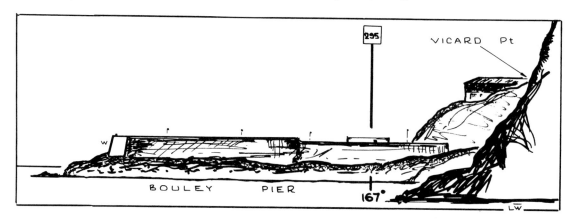

295 root of Bouley Pier × Vicard Point, which clears E of les Sambues. The turn into Bonne Nuit harbour is

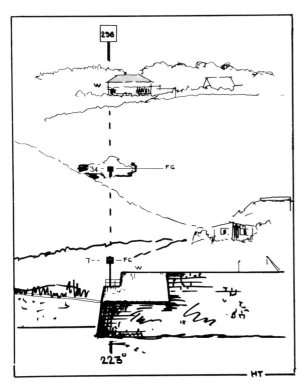

296 a white house × the pier end. At night 2 leading lights take over. Here there is a hotel, a pub, a shop and a bus service to Town (30 minutes). There remains one more anchorage, Grève de Lecq – the harbour is ruined – which is easy to enter (Chart O, p. 50A),

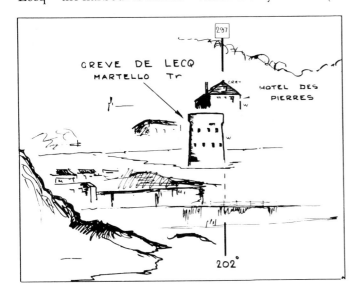

297 Hotel des Pierres × the white Martello tower. A safety clearance from Sorel Point is

145

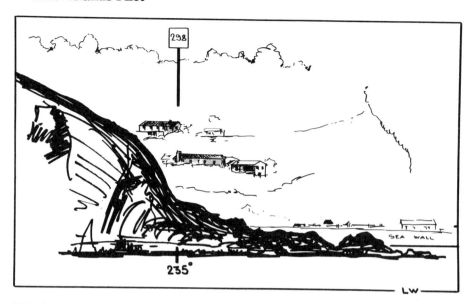

298 the right and left gables of 2 houses × the cliff. Grève de Lecq, apart from a couple of pubs and a distant shop, has little to recommend it. There is a bus to Town every half hour.

Back now to chart Z, p. 42A: clear Grosnez Point by as little as 1ca. and sail SW down the Swashway Channel and the North-west passage, p. 125 and on to Chart N, p. 44A. When about half a mile NW of the Corbière LtHo, look for

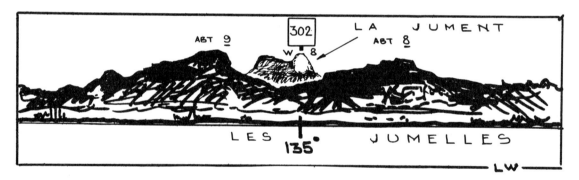

302 a white-painted rock, la Jument, midway between the heads of les Jumelles. This is the lead-in mark for the inshore passage between Noirmontaise and the Corbière (3·0m). When within 2ca. of the Corbière Rock, which is very steep-to, make a handrail southabout 150–200m off, clear la Jument likewise and take the NW passage, **248** (99°) the German tower at Noirmont Point × le Frêt Point, p. 126.

St Brelade's Bay comes next.

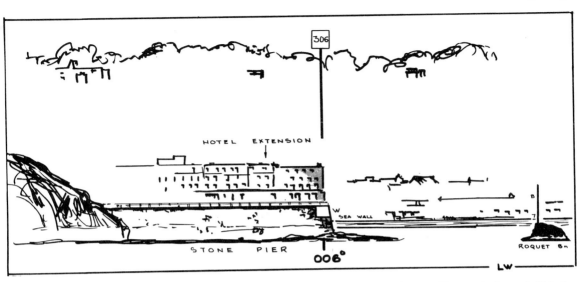

306 The right side of a hotel × the white patch on the pier end. The small area sheltered slightly by the pier dries *3·5m*. The eastern entrance is

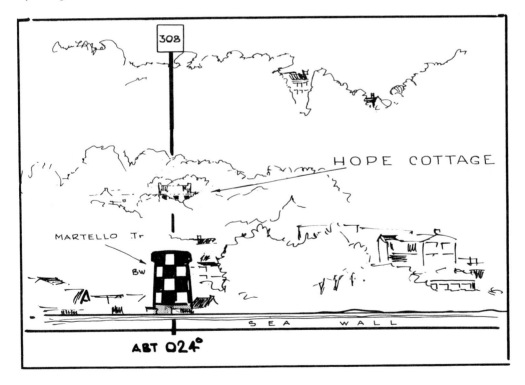

308 a house, 'Hope Cottage', × the chequered Martello tower, which is an old-time 'beaching mark'. The house is partly hidden among trees. On the W side of the bay try

147

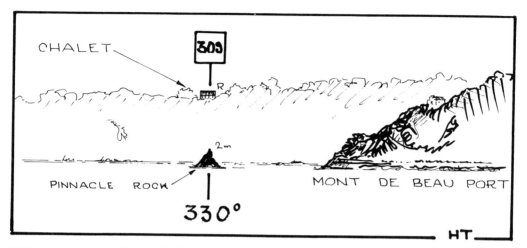

309 a chalet × the Pinnacle Rock, which entices you into Beau Port. This and the next bay, Portelet, are fine for a summer picnic.

Since it is close to Town, the dangers in St Aubin Bay are well marked. To make for St Aubin, use the Sillette passage (p. 128), **253** (000°) Martello tower No.2 × the right side of Grosse Rock, p. 128. Leave the Grosse and Platte Bns, also St Aubin Fort, 1ca. to port and head for the harbour mouth. The short-cut track I shown on Chart N, p. 44A, (335°) crosses the causeway to the Fort – minimum depth 1·0m at half tide. To the SW of the pair of Bns a stone pier is useful for dinghies when the causeway is covered. St Aubin harbour is the yachting centre of Jersey and so has all facilities. The berths for visitors are alongside the NE quay where there are ladders. The first berth on entering dries *6.4m.* The whole harbour is mud. It is the headquarters of the Royal Channel Islands Yacht Club, which offers every hospitality. Frequent buses to Town (15 minutes), calor gas, water by hose, fuel, chandlery.

Bonne Nuit Harbour, Jersey

6 Les Ecrehou

From where we sit, backs to a sun-warmed wall, the Paternosters stand black above the evening horizon. Beside me Alphonse le Gastellois, King of the Ecrehou, tells of blinding fogs and snarling gales, of ormer harvests and conger hunts, massive cray and giant octopus. At the top of the springs our yacht tugs to and fro on her mooring, while the tide seems about to eddy into one house and out of another.

A while back these rocks were a gift to a Norman monastery on condition that a light be built for ships and a chapel for souls. In 1309, 106 years later, the Abbot of Valricher, with Tax Avoidance in mind, proved that the priory of the Ecrehou was maintained by revenue from a mill near Rozel. The money, he said, was essential to pay for a daily mass for the King. And, of course, to maintain the Lighthouse. The Seigneur of the manor of Rozel must have relented and let him off paying *droit de moulinage* for the priory still exists on Maître Île.

Over 100 years ago, when returning to Jersey from France in windless weather, a sailing ship was holed on the reef at low water. The 30 passengers, all women, just managed to crowd on a small rock while the crew swam to safety on Marmotière. Night fell. The tide rose. When morning came the rock was bare. Carried on a sullen winter's gale the screams can still be heard when the spring tides wash over a rock with the name Prières des Femmes.

And there is still no light on the Ecrehou.

From Rozel to the Ecrehou is only 5 miles and it isn't surprising that, though smaller than the Minquiers, the island is visited more often. The houses, about a dozen, are well kept and their States leases are much prized by Jersey yachtsmen.

The best time to arrive is about half-tide down, when the current is flowing NW and after a bearing or so taken on the house on Maître Île the first mark will be seen.

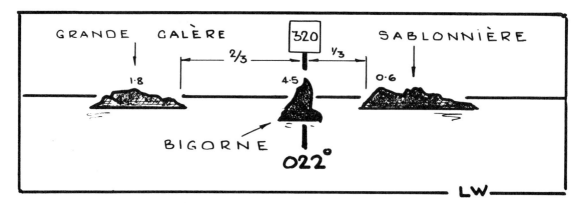

320 Bigorne between Grande Galère and Sablonnière (Chart U, p. 52A). The second mark leads to the anchorage,

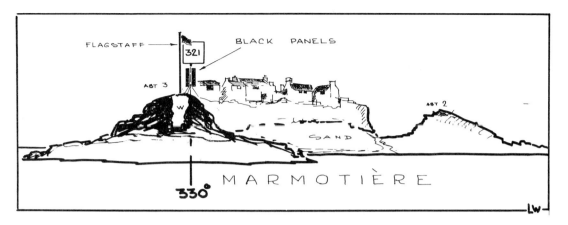

321 2 black panels × the flagstaff. When abreast of the N end of Maître Île, borrow a bit to the NE as shown. You will find a states of Jersey mooring buoy ½ca. SSE of the flagpole.

There is a pool with a sandy bottom about 2ca. WSW of Marmotière, where one or 2 local yachts have moorings, in 1·2m. When Pommère *3·2m* is covered it is safe to shift from the States anchorage on the track shown on Chart U. This leaves Marmotière a metre or so to stb'd; past the W end of the slip, then SW where the moorings can be seen. The tide starts to run SE at about low water, the general rate being 4 knots. But between rocks, at springs, this can easily be doubled for a short time therefore stick to neaps for a first visit. Power, to all but the foolhardy, is essential. So is daylight and settled weather – after all, the Prières des Femmes is still there.

7 PLATEAU DES MINQUIERS

When I first visited what the locals call the Minkies, it was a still, autumn day. Our boat safely at anchor, my companion went ormering while I climbed to the top of Maîtresse Île. Five miles away to the W the Maisons Bns made a crown for its lion's head. The 2 of us were the only humans crawling about on these 25 square miles of pinnacle, sand bar and tombstone. A pale sun washed the pond-dead sea as in an empty well. In another 6 hours the picture would be turned back to front – rock heads leaving a slick on the mill race of the tide, the warm sand now down in the chill weed-strewn depths. Perhaps a thin fog drifts in from the E, dissolving the Bns. Or maybe a coming blow from the N grinds the swell into foam. Yes, I see the dinghy still safely tied – better get going if we want to be clear of this lot before dark.

Compared with the Ecrehou, the Minkies are less visited though better marked. No longer inhabited, the area is 10 times as big. For the adventurous? Yes – but you must have one or 2 things right first. Settled weather and light winds; to be caught out in a blow could be serious. Visibility must be more than 1½ miles; night work is out. Whilst Admiralty chart 3656 is most useful, there are many more heads than are shown. Chart T must be used with caution also, and I was in two minds whether to draw in the usual 3m contour. However my line at least includes the trouble spots. Oh, one more item: an engine – one unlikely to stop.

151

Try to time your arrival not earlier than half-tide down, which at springs means that most of the day can be spent ashore. Neaps are less traumatic, but this means an afternoon high water, so you may have to do without the breakwater provided by those 25 square miles of rockware. Probably your first visit will be from Jersey (technically you must clear there first) and in any case the southern approach is difficult to identify.

A century ago quarrymen built and lived in the dozen small stone houses, and for generations French and Jersey fishermen shared the harvest of the Minkies. Victor Hugo mentions them in the *Toilers of the Sea*, and Hammond Innes's novel, the *Wreck of the Mary Deare*, is set there. Post-war, though hardly a Struggle for Power, the sovereignty of the reef was decided between France and Britain at the Hague in 1953.

France lost her case and immediately whipped away all her magnificent buoys, leaving the States of Jersey to cope as best they could. Their old names like Brisants du Sud, Caux and les Sauvages gave way to dull though more explicit point of the compass.

From St Helier it is 10 miles, and a useful departing mark is **255** (350°) power station chimney × Demi de Pas Lt for as long as you can see it. The passage is free of all dangers. The key to the entrance from the northward is the Demie de Vascelin unlit green buoy with a radar top. It must be left just to the W when you can start sorting out from the maze of rocks spanning the southern horizon the first mark.

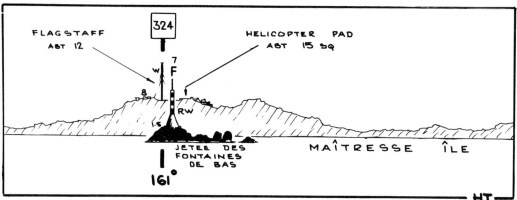

324 Flagstaff × Jetée des Fontaines de Bas Bn. At 1ca. from the Bn come to stb'd on

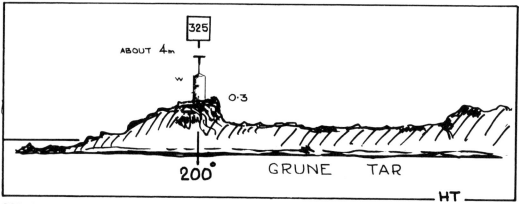

325 Grune Tar Bn at 200°. Now straighten the dog-leg,

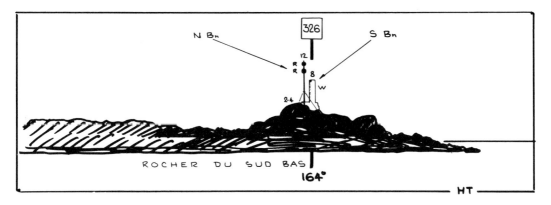

326 the 2 Rocher du Sud Bas Bns in line. Both Bns are on the same rock and only 25m apart. Round Les Demics (drawn on Chart T, p. 52A) 1ca. off and head E,

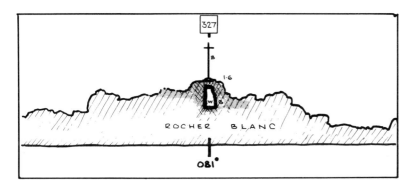

327 the 2 Rocher Blanc Bns in line. From now on it is all drying.

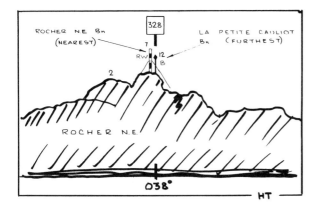

328 La Petite Gauliot Bn × Rocher NE Bn. Either anchor when the States beacon bears 015°, or use the States of Jersey buoy at the same position, in the middle of the anchorage. This is laid for

153

the States tug of 80 tons when on buoyage duty and it has triple mooring chains. If drying out, the bottom is soft sand and mud, so don't fix legs. Now is the time to relax and decide whether to clear off on the rising tide or stop the night. Why not spend a day or so exploring this fascinating area? At low water most movement stops and a dinghy can be taken among the sand bars to your own uninhabited desert island. The strongest current, 4 knots, is about 2 hours before high water, direction SE, so the States anchorage is reasonably sheltered. Long before this you must be aboard your boat, for at springs only a powerful outboard would save you a scare. The States of Jersey have thoughtfully installed a refuge hut – white column 6m high topped by a 2m-square white hut with a ladder – with food, water and clothes, at Pipette rock, 49°00·0′ 2°10·0′ and on Maîtresse Île there is a helicopter pad. This is an Anglo-French realization in concrete 50m square, and alongside is built another store of food, water, etc., for emergency use.

Ashore on Maîtresse Île are a dozen stone houses, now occupied mostly by shags. There doesn't seem to be the same desire to populate here as in the Ecrehou. Landing is at the 80m-long slip NW of the States mooring buoy.

The States Bn was built mainly to clinch territorial rights – it is better than the official flagstaff, as a noticeboard demonstrates. It is in French and English.

17.9.1947

Fishermen who have built this cabin have taken the engagement to respect the British flag which flies nearby, and have always respected it. Visitors are asked to do the same.

Notice is hereby given that should the French national emblem be once more taken down from its flagpole and carried away, the British ensign shall likewise. And whenever it will fly, be removed until matters are settled through a definite international agreement. Private interference is from every point of view unwelcome.

The French flagstaff today remains some 100m to the SW of that of the States of Jersey – forlorn, unpainted and forgotten.

In 1800 the quarrymen, busy hacking stone for Fort Regent, St Helier, had had enough. By 1807 they had petitioned the Governor of Jersey to let them stop work before they were swept away. He didn't agree, so the men emigrated to Chausey to work for the French. Until just before World War II, fishermen from la Roque, Jersey, reckoned the Minkies were their exclusive grounds. Then was the time the famous Marin-Marie, Chausey yachtsmen and painter, built the French cabin that started the squabble about sovereignty.

Should you want to sail on southwards instead of going back to Jersey, leave about an hour before low water. Retrace your route along the last 2 marks, **328** (038°) la Petite Gauliot Bn × Rocher NE Bn and **327** (081°) the 2 Rocher Blanc Bns in line. Then turn SE,

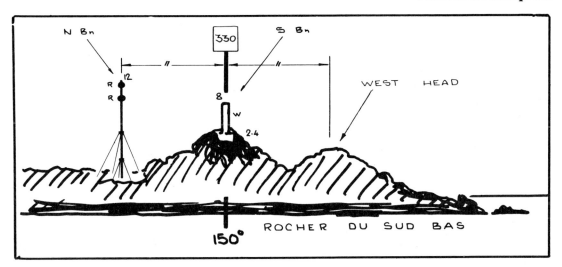

330 the 2 Rocher du Sud Bas Bns open to the W. When 1ca. short of these 2 Bns, make a handrail westabout until they are exactly in line behind you. This is of course the reciprocal of view **326**. This mark takes you clear out to sea, but it must be held accurately for at least 3 miles, which is why the approach from the S isn't easy to locate. Pass E of the SE Minquiers buoy – there are drying rocks 4ca. North-westwards. From here to St Malo is only 14 miles. . . I'll see you on the Quai St Louis!

Index

Positions of places named in the text are given in minutes of latitude and longitude. Whole degress are omitted for clarity, as the degree of latitude is 49 N, except where the minutes exceed 50·0, when the degree is 48 N; the degree of longitude is 2 W, except where the minutes exceed 50·0, when the degree is 1 W.

Thus Fort Albert is 49°43·7′N, 2°10·9′W; Brett Bn is 49°08·9′N, 1°58·8′W.

See page 18 for a full description of these charts.
(See inside front cover to complete tidal cycle.)